HISPANIC AMERICANS:
A Statistical Sourcebook

2002 Edition

Louise L. Hornor
Editor

information
publications

REF
E
184
.S75
H5655
2002

ISBN 0-929960-33-5

© 2002 Information Publications

printed in the United States of America

All Rights Reserved. No part of this book may be reproduced or transmitted in any
form or by any means whatsoever, including photocopying, recording, or in any information storage and retrieval system, without permission in writing from the publisher.

Printed on recycled paper.

Information Publications
3790 El Camino Real, PMB 162
Palo Alto, CA 94306
phone: 408-286-4449
fax: 408-297-3770
www.InformationPublications.com

HISPANIC AMERICANS:
A Statistical Sourcebook

Introduction xi

Table of Contents

Chapter 4 - Education: Preprimary through High School   51

Chapter 5 - Education: Postsecondary & Educational Attainment   69

Chapter 6 - Government & Elections 91

Chapter 7 - The Labor Force, Employment & Unemployment 107

Table of Contents

Chapter 9 - Crime & Corrections

Chapter 10 - Special Topics

Table of Contents

Introduction

Hispanic Americans: A Statistical Sourcebook is the third in a series of statistical sourcebooks covering significant topics in American life and the second in this series designed as an annual publication. This is its twelfth edition. Hispanic Americans resulted from the view that, despite the fact that there is coverage of Hispanic Americans in an assortment of reference sources, there is a need for a single volume statistical reference devoted entirely to this important segment of the population.

Hispanic Americans provides an extensive collection of tables which display information on a wide variety of topics. With a few exceptions, each table presents information about the Hispanic population, the White population, and a total for Americans of all races and ethnic groups. The purpose in doing so is not to advance a specific perspective about Hispanic Americans but to provide a context within which the tabular data can be more fully understood and evaluated.

It is essential to understand before using this book that Hispanics (as viewed by most federal data collection agencies) are **not** a racial group. They are the only ethnic or cultural group on which the federal government gathers data. Persons of Hispanic origin may be Hispanic and white, or Hispanic and black, or Hispanic and Asian, etc. As a general guideline, the overwhelming majority of persons who identify themselves as Hispanic also identify themselves as white for federal data collection purposes.

Presenting data by race and ethnicity always puts one at risk of being labeled racist. Although undoubtedly there will be persons on both sides - those who see Hispanic Americans as a propagandistic derogation of the Hispanic community and those who feel that the book eloquently proves the inherent prejudice of our culture - the intent here is to serve neither cause. In fact, Hispanic Americans is not intended to serve any cause or advance any point of view but to serve as a reportorial resource, providing access to federal government information. By researching and presenting this sometimes difficult to find, hard to understand information, Hispanic Americans can serve students, business persons, social scientists, researchers, and others who need basic data about Hispanic Americans.

The use of the term 'Hispanic' itself can also be a cause for controversy. A number of terms have been used by Hispanic Americans to name themselves, such as Latino and Spanish. Hispanic is used here solely because it is the word currently used by the federal government in gathering data. In some surveys, data is further analyzed into subgroups of the Hispanic population (e.g., Mexican Americans, Cuban-Americans, etc.). Where such data is available in this detail, it is presented here.

Another sensitive question is, who is Hispanic? For federal data collection purposes, Hispanic persons are those who say they are Hispanic (or, Spanish, Latino, etc.). For statistical reporting purposes, being Hispanic is based solely on the self-identification of the respondent.

As was stated, most agencies of the federal government consider Hispanic to be a supplement to racial categories. However, some agencies collect data as if Hispanic origin was a racial category. For example, the Centers for Disease Control collects data about AIDS using the classifications of White non-Hispanic, Black non-Hispanic, and Hispanic. The Department of Education also collects data in this manner. These agencies are the exception to the rule, and such exceptions are noted in the table notes at the end of each table.

Organization

The main portion of this book has been divided into ten chapters of tables:

Chapter 1:	Demographics
Chapter 2:	Social Characteristics
Chapter 3:	Household & Family Characteristics
Chapter 4:	Education: Preprimary through High School
Chapter 5:	Education: Postsecondary & Educational Attainment
Chapter 6:	Government & Elections
Chapter 7:	The Labor Force, Employment & Unemployment
Chapter 8:	Earnings, Income, Poverty, & Wealth
Chapter 9:	Crime & Corrections
Chapter 10:	Special Topics

The tables in each chapter represent results of a comprehensive review of all available federal government statistical information on the Hispanic population. This material was edited and organized into chapters and arranged in a sequence roughly following the pattern found in publications of the U.S. Bureau of the Census.

Each table presents pertinent information from the source or sources in a clear, comprehensible fashion. As users of this book will likely be a diverse group ranging from librarians to business planners, from social scientists to marketers, all with different uses for the same data, the information selected for presentation was chosen for its broad scope and general appeal.

The Sources

All of the information in Hispanic Americans comes from U.S. Government sources either originally or by way of republication by the federal government. In turn, most of the federal information is from the U.S. Bureau of the Census. Without question, the Bureau is the largest data gathering organization in the nation. It collects information on an exceptionally broad range of topics, not only for its own use and for the use of Congress and the Executive, but also for other federal agencies and departments. The reach of the Bureau is wider than most people realize. It encompasses the decennial Census of Population, the Current Population Survey, and the Annual Housing Survey. In cooperation with other agencies, the Bureau extends to the Consumer Expenditure Survey, the National Crime Survey, the National Family Growth Survey, and many others. The fact that the Bureau is responsible for so much of the federal government's data collection adds uniformity to the statistical information published by different agencies. Although the uniformity is not complete, there is enough to make the work of data users a lot easier. The influence of the Bureau of the Census extends beyond federal government data collection. Because of the sheer volume of data it collects, many private data collectors have adopted some of its procedures and terminology. This has the added value for researchers of making private and public data more compatible.

Observant readers will note that the source of many tables is a Census publication, Statistical Abstract of the United States. There are a number of reasons for this. First, due to federal budget cuts, a growing quantity of information used in <u>Statistical Abstract</u> has never been published elsewhere before or it has never been published in such a detailed way. Second, as the preeminent federal data publisher, the Census Bureau has access to a wealth of raw data in machine readable form. It is able to aggregate data geographically on regional lines and break out other detail such as age, sex, race, etc., using its own parameters for publication. Thus, even when information is published elsewhere, the manner of presentation in <u>Statistical Abstract</u> is likely to be unique. Data from this source is presented in a more general way so as to be useful to many different types of data users.

On all tables where <u>Statistical Abstract</u> is cited as the source, the original source also has been checked for additional information. To make more detailed research easier, <u>Statistical Abstract's</u> own source (if it is not the Bureau itself), is listed as well.

Types of Information

Regardless of its source, there are basically two types of data presented in the tables of this book.

The first is complete count data. For example, the five questions asked of all Americans by the Bureau of the Census in its decennial census was an attempt at a complete count of a given universe.

The second type of data is survey information. Here a fairly large, specifically chosen segment of a population is studied. This sample is drawn to be statistically representative of the entire population or universe. Information about housing units and money income are some of the items in this book based on this type of survey information. Of course, survey information is only as good as the survey itself; therefore, the reader should always be the judge of the significance and accuracy of the material presented as it applies to his or her own research. Although specific survey methodology is not discussed here, a full reference to each source is made on every table. Interested readers may consult the original source materials, which in most cases contain a detailed explanation of survey methodology.

The Tables

This section details how the tables have been prepared and presented. Table titles are the first source of valuable information:

Table 4.01   School Enrollment, by Age, 2000

The table number contains the chapter number to the left of the decimal and the location of the table within the chapter to the right of the decimal. Thus Table 4.01 is the first table of Chapter 4. With a few exceptions, tables have been arranged within a chapter to present the oldest, most general information first, followed by newer, more specific information. This pattern is mirrored in the tables themselves, which present the oldest, most general information at the beginning.

In a table title, the word or words before the first comma identify the general topic of the table. Following the first comma is descriptive wording which identifies the detail presented about the general topic; i.e., the data is presented by age, sex, marital status, etc., in this case, by age. After the description of the presentation of the data, the years for which data is presented are shown.

It should be noted that both the table titles and the tables themselves retain the original terms of the source material. This has the advantage of making the book compatible with the original sources.

To further facilitate use, every table in the book presents data in two, three, five, or six columns. The left-most column or columns are for the Hispanic population; the center column or columns are for the White population; and the right-hand column or columns present data for all races and/or ethnic groups. For data which is available in subgroups of the Hispanic population, a separate six column table is provided, with columns for Hispanics of Mexican origin, Puerto Rican origin, Cuban origin, Central/South American origin, other Hispanic origin, and a total of all persons of Hispanic origin.

Along the left margin of each table appears a column of line descriptors. Here, after a general heading, subgroups of the heading (usually indented) are shown. Two principles cover arranging and presenting the line descriptors: the oldest, most general information appears first, progressing to the newer, more specific; and quantities appear first, followed by percentages, medians, means, and per capita amounts.

Wherever available and appropriate, a time span of data is presented, usually going back five to ten years. This provides readers with a historical context for the information. However, readers should be cautioned that the years selected have been chosen from no special knowledge of the subject, nor to make any specific point. Thus the fact that there has been a decrease or increase in a given indicator for the period displayed does not mean that the same trend will continue, or that it represents the continuation of a historical trend, or even that which appears to be a trend within this period actually is one. The time span and specific dates have been chosen largely to create a congruity of data, and a basis of comparison between different categories of information.

Table Notes

At the bottom of each table three key paragraphs appear: Source, Notes, and Units. The **Source** paragraph lists the source of the data presented in the table. When more than one source was used, the sources are listed in the same order in which the data itself appears in the table. As all sources are government publications, the issuing agency is listed as the author. All citations provide both the page and table number in the source from which the material was taken. This bibliographic detail on each table makes a separate bibliography at the end of the book unnecessary. A Superintendent of Documents Classification Number is also provided. This number is used as a locator number in most government depository libraries, and documents are shelved or filed according to it, just the way books in some public libraries are organized by the Dewey Decimal System.

An increasing number of sources are now available on the internet, and in many cases, only on the internet. For tables pulled exclusively from on-line sources, the Universal Resource Locator (URL) is listed as the source.

The paragraph of **Notes** includes pertinent facts about the data, the time of year covered by the survey, and the scope of the survey universe. In those cases where Hispanic origin is a separate race-like category (i.e., where the data is collected in such a way that one can be either Hispanic or white, but not both), this is stated. One general note can be made here at the outset about all tabular data: detail (subgroups) may not add to the total shown, due to either rounding or the fact that only selected subgroups are displayed.

The final paragraph of a table, **Units,** identifies the units used, specifically stating that the quantity is millions of persons, thousands of workers, dollars per capita, etc. Readers are urged to pay special attention to this especially when a median, mean, percent, rate, or a per capita amount is provided.

The Index

Every key term from the tables has been indexed. Readers should note that the index provides table numbers as opposed to page numbers.

The Glossary

It is important to be clear about terminology in a work such as this. Not only does the government have overtly specialized terms which clearly require a definition or explanation, but many government agencies use ordinary words in specialized ways. There are real differences between: a household and a family; a family and a married couple; the resident population and the civilian non-institutional population; a service industry and a service occupation; an urban area and a metropolitan area; to name just a few. All specialized terms are defined either in the table or in the glossary. Needless to say, it is absolutely vital to understand the meaning of all terms used in a table before drawing any conclusions from the data. When in doubt, consult the glossary.

For many tables, it is not possible to fully define a term or concept in the table notes, so the glossary serves as an important tool in using the tables. All terms that appear in either the title or text of a table which may be unclear or are used in a special way are defined in the glossary. Wherever possible, the definition is adapted (and in many cases taken verbatim) from the definition provided in the source publication. Not all source materials provide definitions, so sometimes a definition has been constructed by reviewing and summarizing explanatory and supplementary material from the source.

In compiling the glossary the intention was to provide short clear definitions, including only as much background material as necessary to make a term understandable. However, in practice this resulted in compromises. For certain terms (such as metropolitan area concepts), some methodological background is essential in order to achieve an understanding. Where such background is vital it has been included. Readers requiring additional technical or methodological detail are referred to the sources for more complete explanations.

A Suggestion on How to Use This Book

One way to use this book is by locating the subject of general interest in the Table of Contents, and turning to that chapter. While the Table of Contents is detailed enough to narrow a search and the index can speed access to specific items, sometimes paging through the dozen or so tables in a given field uncovers unanticipated information of genuine importance. It is just this type of serendipity that has lead to the inclusion of information in this book, and sometimes such an unexpected find can greatly enhance a research project.

A Final Word

As this book is updated on an annual basis, questions, comments, and criticisms from users are vital to making informed editorial choices about succeeding editions. If you have a suggestion or comment, be assured that it will be both appreciated and carefully considered. If you should find an error here, please let us know so that it may be corrected. Our goal is to provide accurate, easy to use, statistical compendiums which serve our readers' needs. Your help enables us to do our job better.

Chapter 1: Demographics

Table 1.01 Resident Population and Median Age, 1980 - 2000

| | Hispanic | | White | | Total | |
	total	median age	total	median age	total	median age
1980 (April 1)	14,609	23.2	194,713	30.9	226,546	30.0
1985 (July 1)	17,865	na	202,769	32.4	235,736	31.4
1986 (July 1)	18,523	na	204,326	32.7	241,096	31.7
1987 (July 1)	19,183	25.1	205,833	33.0	243,400	32.1
1988 (July 1)	19,847	25.8	207,357	33.1	245,807	32.3
1989 (July 1)	20,505	26.1	208,961	33.6	248,240	32.7
1990 (April 1)	22,354	na	199,686	na	248,710	32.8
1991 (July 1)	23,350	25.7	210,899	34.1	252,177	33.1
1992 (July 1)	24,238	25.8	212,912	34.4	255,082	33.4
1994 (July 1)	26,077	26.1	216,470	35.0	260,341	34.0
1995 (July 1)	26,994	26.2	218,085	35.3	262,755	34.3
1996 (July 1)	28,269	26.4	219,749	35.7	265,284	34.6
1997 (July 1)	29,348	26.4	221,334	36.0	267,636	34.9
1998 (July 1)	30,250	26.4	223,001	36.3	270,299	35.2
1999 (July 1)	31,337	26.5	224,611	36.6	272,691	35.5
2000 (April)	35,306	na	211,461	na	281,422	na

SOURCE: U.S. Bureau of the Census, Statistical Abstract of the United States, 1989, p. 17, table 21; 1990; p. 17, table 19; 1991; p. 17, table 19; 1993; p. 14, table 12; p. 15, table 14, page 23, table 24; 1994, pp. 22-23, table 22; 1995, pp. 22-23, table 22; 1996, pp. 22-23, table 22; 1997, pp. 22-23, table 22; 1998, pp. 22-23, table 22; 1999, pp. 22-23, table 22; 2000, pp. 20-21, table 19; 2001; p. 24, table 22. C 3.134:(year)

NOTES: 'Total' includes other races and ethnic groups not shown separately.

UNITS: Population in thousands of persons; median age in years.

Table 1.02   Resident Population, by Age and Sex, 1998, 1999

	Hispanic	White	Total
1998			
Both sexes			
total	30,250	223,001	270,299
under 5 years old	3,393	15,052	18,966
5-13 years old	5,219	27,907	35,389
14-17 years old	2,122	12,284	15,517
85 years old and older	177	3,666	4,054
male			
total	15,233	109,489	132,046
under 5 years old	1,733	7,712	9,696
5-13 years old	2,663	14,304	18,114
14-17 years old	1,099	6,336	7,985
85 years old and older	59	1,066	1,187
female			
total	15,017	113,511	138,252
under 5 years old	1,660	7,340	9,270
5-13 years old	2,556	13,603	17,275
14-17 years old	1,023	5,948	7,532
85 years old and older	118	2,600	2,866
1999			
total	31,337	224,611	272,691
under 5 years old	3,467	15,043	18,942
5-13 years old	5,451	28,019	35,603
14-17 years old	2,167	12,380	15,654
85 years old and older	189	3,773	4,175

SOURCE: U.S. Bureau of the Census, <u>Statistical Abstract of the United States, 1999</u>, p. 21, table 21; <u>2000</u>; p. 13, table 12; p. 15, table 14; p. 18, table 17, p. 19, table 18 (data from US. Bureau of the Census, *Current Population Reports*, Series P-25). C 3.134:(year)

NOTES: 'Total' includes other races and ethnic groups not shown separately.

UNITS: Resident population in thousands of persons.

Table 1.03 Hispanic Population, by Type of Origin, by Age, 2000

	Mexican	Puerto Rican	Cuban	Central/ South American	Other Hispanic	Total Hispanic
2000						
Total population	100.0%	100.0%	100.0%	100.0%	100.0%	100.0%
Under 5 years old	12.4	9.4	5.1	8.5	10.2	11.2
5-9 years old	10.9	9.7	4.6	8.9	9.9	10.2
10-14 years old	9.6	9.6	5.4	7.7	9.4	10.2
15-19 years old	9.2	9.4	6.0	7.8	8.1	9.1
20-24 years old	8.9	7.4	4.7	8.7	6.2	8.4
25-29 years old	9.1	7.5	4.8	8.6	7.6	8.6
30-34 years old	8.5	8.9	8.0	9.3	7.9	8.6
35-44 years old	14.2	14.5	17.0	19.0	15.9	15.2
45-54 years old	8.4	10.4	12.9	10.4	10.6	9.2
55-64 years old	4.3	7.2	10.5	6.3	7.4	5.3
65-74 years old	2.8	4.0	12.2	3.2	4.3	3.4
75-84 years old	1.2	1.9	7.2	1.2	1.8	1.6
85 years and over	0.2	0.1	1.6	0.3	0.8	0.3

SOURCE: U.S. Bureau of the Census, "Current Population Reports: The Hispanic Population of the United States, 2000, (Table) 1.1. Population by Sex, Age, Hispanic Origin, and Race: March 2000;" published 6 March 2001, <http://www.census.gov/population/socdemo/hispanic/p20-535/tab01-1.txt>

NOTES: Total population includes other races and ethnic groups not shown separately. 'Other Hispanic origin' includes persons from Spain and persons identifying themselves generally as Hispanic, Spanish, Spanish-American, Hispano, Latino, etc.

UNITS: Percent as a percent of total shown (100.0%).

Table 1.04 Hispanic Population, by Type of Origin, by Sex, 2000

	male	female	both sexes
2000			
Total Hispanic population	16,435	16,369	32,804
by origin			
Mexican origin	11,120	10,582	21,701
Puerto Rican origin	1,463	1,496	2,959
Cuban origin	631	669	1,300
Central/South American origin	2,216	2,526	4,743
other Hispanic origin	1,005	1,095	2,101

SOURCE: U.S. Bureau of the Census, "Current Population Reports: The Hispanic Population of the United States, 2000, (Table 1). "Selected Summary Measures of Age and Income by Hispanic Origin and Race: March 2000" published March 6, 2001, <http://www.census.gov/population/socdemo/hispanic/p20-535/sumtab01.txt>

NOTES: 'Other Hispanic origin' includes persons from Spain and persons identifying themselves generally as Hispanic, Spanish, Spanish-American, Hispano, Latino, etc.

UNITS: Resident population in percent, by sex, as a percent of all persons.

Table 1.05   Population Projections, by Age, 2005

	Hispanic	White	Total
2005			
total	38,189	234,221	287,716
under 5 years	4,027	15,041	19,212
5 to 9 years	3,681	15,074	19,122
10 to 14 years	3,622	16,077	20,634
15 to 19 years	3,307	16,405	20,990
20 to 24 years	3,224	15,965	20,159
25 to 29 years	3,011	14,490	18,351
35 to 34 years	2,888	14,642	18,582
35 to 39 years	2,851	16,049	20,082
40 to 44 years	2,767	18,447	22,634
45 to 49 years	2,278	18,354	22,230
50 to 54 years	1,778	16,429	19,661
55 to 59 years	1,352	14,334	16,842
60 to 64 years	989	11,022	12,848
65 to 69 years	770	8,621	10,086
70 to 74 years	599	7,270	8,375
75 to 79 years	470	6,563	7,429
80 to 84 years	308	4,972	5,514
85 to 89 years	155	2,746	3,028
90 to 94 years	78	1,257	1,402
95 to 99 years	27	386	442
100 years old and over	7	78	96

SOURCE: U.S. Bureau of the Census, Statistical Abstract of the United States, 2001; p. 15, table 13; p. 18, table 16; p. 19, table 17, p. 19, table 17(data from US. Bureau of the Census, *Current Population Reports*, Series P-25). C 3.134:001

NOTES: 'Total' includes other races and ethnic groups not shown separately. Population projections as of July 1, of the year shown.

UNITS: Estimates of the total population in thousands of persons, includes armed forces overseas. Based on Series 14 - Middle Series.

Table 1.06   Population Projections, by Sex, 2000 - 2025

	Hispanic	White	Total
2000			
both sexes	31,366	225,532	274,634
male	15,799	110,799	134,181
female	15,566	114,734	140,453
2005			
both sexes	36,057	232,463	285,981
male	18,082	114,350	139,785
female	17,975	118,113	146,196
2010			
both sexes	41,139	239,588	297,716
male	20,557	118,000	145,584
female	20,582	121,588	152,132
2025			
both sexes	58,930	262,227	335,050
male	29,276	129,596	164,119
female	29,654	132,631	170,931

SOURCE: U.S. Bureau of the Census, <u>Statistical Abstract of the United States</u>, <u>1996</u>; p. 25, table 24; p. 26, table 25; (data from U.S. Bureau of the Census, *Current Population Reports*, Series P-25). C 3.134:996

NOTES: 'Total' includes other races and ethnic groups not shown separately. Population projections as of July 1, of the year shown.

UNITS: Estimates of the total population in thousands of persons, includes armed forces overseas. Based on Series 14 - Middle Series.

Table 1.07   Population Projections, 1999 - 2100 (revised)

	Hispanic	White	Total
1999	31,355	224,650	272,820
2000	32,478	226,265	275,306
2005	38,188	234,221	287,715
2010	43,687	241,769	299,861
2015	49,255	249,467	312,268
2020	55,156	257,394	324,926
2025	61,433	265,305	337,814
2030	68,167	273,079	351,070
2035	75,289	280,555	364,319
2040	82,691	287,786	377,349
2045	90,343	295,019	390,397
2050	98,228	302,453	403,686
2055	106,370	310,300	417,477
2060	114,796	318,752	432,010
2065	123,508	327,907	447,415
2070	132,492	337,719	463,639
2075	141,719	348,027	480,504
2080	151,154	358,664	497,829
2085	160,763	369,547	515,528
2090	170,514	380,674	533,605
2095	180,377	392,063	552,085
2100	190,330	403,696	570,954

SOURCE: U.S. Bureau of the Census, <u>Projections of the Resident Population by Race, Hispanic Origin, and Nativity: Middle Series, 1999 to 2100</u> Tables NP-T5-A - NP-T5-H
<www.census.gov/population/www/projections/natproj.html> accessed 1 February 2000

NOTES: 'Total' includes other races and ethnic groups not shown separately. Population projections as of July 1, of the year shown.

UNITS: Estimates of the total population in thousands of persons, includes armed forces overseas. Based on Series 14 - Middle Series.

Table 1.08   Resident Population, by State, 1980

	Hispanic	White	Total
Alabama	34	2,873	3,894
Alaska	9	310	402
Arizona	444	2,241	2,718
Arkansas	17	1,890	2,286
California	4,541	18,031	23,668
Colorado	341	2,571	2,890
Connecticut	125	2,799	3,108
Delaware	10	488	594
District of Columbia	18	172	638
Florida	585	8,185	9,746
Georgia	61	3,947	5,463
Hawaii	71	319	965
Idaho	37	902	944
Illinois	635	9,233	11,427
Indiana	87	5,004	5,490
Iowa	26	2,839	2,914
Kansas	63	2,168	2,364
Kentucky	27	3,379	3,661
Louisiana	100	2,912	4,206
Maine	5	1,110	1,125
Maryland	63	3,159	4,217
Massachusetts	141	5,363	5,737
Michigan	158	7,872	9,262
Minnesota	32	3,936	4,076
Mississippi	24	1,615	2,521
Missouri	52	4,345	4,917
Montana	10	740	787
Nebraska	28	1,490	1,570
Nevada	54	700	800
New Hampshire	5	910	921
New Jersey	494	6,127	7,365
New Mexico	477	978	1,303
New York	1,661	13,961	17,558

continued on the next page

Table 1.08   continued

	Hispanic	White	Total
North Carolina	56	4,458	5,882
North Dakota	3	626	653
Ohio	120	9,597	10,798
Oklahoma	58	2,598	3,025
Oregon	66	2,491	2,633
Pennsylvania	154	10,652	11,864
Rhode Island	19	897	947
South Carolina	34	2,147	3,122
South Dakota	4	640	691
Tennessee	34	3,835	4,591
Texas	2,983	11,198	14,229
Utah	60	1,383	1,461
Vermont	3	507	511
Virginia	80	4,230	5,347
Washington	121	3,779	4,132
West Virginia	13	1,875	1,950
Wisconsin	63	4,443	4,706
Wyoming	25	446	470

SOURCE: U.S. Bureau of the Census, Census of Population: General Population
Characteristics: United States Summary PC80-1-B1; p. 1-125, table 62.
C 3.223/6:980/B1
U.S. Bureau of the Census, Census of Population: General Social and
Economic Characteristics: United States Summary PC80-1-C1; p. 1-280,
table 233.   C 3.223/7:980/C1

NOTES: 'Total' includes other races and ethnic groups not shown separately.

UNITS: Population in thousands of persons.

Table 1.09　　　　　Resident Population, by State, 1990

	Hispanic	White	Total
Alabama	25	2,976	4,041
Alaska	18	415	550
Arizona	688	2,963	3,665
Arkansas	20	1,945	2,351
California	7,688	20,524	29,760
Colorado	424	2,905	3,294
Connecticut	213	2,859	3,287
Delaware	16	535	666
District of Columbia	33	180	607
Florida	1,574	10,749	12,938
Georgia	109	4,600	6,478
Hawaii	81	370	1,108
Idaho	53	950	1,007
Illinois	904	8,953	11,431
Indiana	99	5,021	5,544
Iowa	33	2,683	2,777
Kansas	94	2,232	2,478
Kentucky	22	3,392	3,685
Louisiana	93	2,839	4,220
Maine	7	1,208	1,228
Maryland	125	3,394	4,781
Massachusetts	288	5,405	6,016
Michigan	202	7,756	9,295
Minnesota	54	4,130	4,375
Mississippi	16	1,633	2,573
Missouri	62	4,486	5,117
Montana	12	741	799
Nebraska	37	1,481	1,578
Nevada	124	1,013	1,202
New Hampshire	11	1,087	1,109
New Jersey	740	6,130	7,730
New Mexico	579	1,146	1,515

continued on the next page

Table 1.09   continued

	Hispanic	White	Total
New York	2,214	13,385	17,990
North Carolina	77	5,008	6,629
North Dakota	5	604	639
Ohio	140	9,522	10,847
Oklahoma	86	2,584	3,146
Oregon	113	2,637	2,842
Pennsylvania	232	10,520	11,882
Rhode Island	46	917	1,003
South Carolina	31	2,407	3,487
South Dakota	5	638	696
Tennessee	33	4,048	4,877
Texas	4,340	12,775	16,987
Utah	85	1,616	1,723
Vermont	4	555	563
Virginia	160	4,792	6,187
Washington	215	4,309	4,867
West Virginia	8	1,792	1,856
Wisconsin	93	4,513	4,892
Wyoming	26	427	454

SOURCE: U.S. Bureau of the Census, Statistical Abstract of the United States, 1991; p. 22, table 27 (data from U.S. Bureau of the Census, *Press Release CB91-100.* C 3.134:991

NOTES: 'Total' includes other races and ethnic groups not shown separately.

UNITS: Population in thousands of persons.

Table 1.10   Population of Cities with 250,000 or More Inhabitants,
2000

	Hispanic	White	Total
Albuquerque, NM	179.1	321.2	448.6
Anaheim, CA	153.4	179.6	328.0
Anchorage, AK	14.8	188.0	260.3
Arlington, TX	60.8	225.4	333.0
Atlanta, GA	18.7	138.4	416.5
Aurora, CO	54.8	190.3	276.4
Austin, TX	200.6	429.1	656.6
Baltimore, MD	11.1	206.0	651.2
Boston, MA	85.1	320.9	589.1
Buffalo, NY	22.1	159.3	292.6
Charlotte, NC	39.8	315.1	540.8
Chicago, IL	753.6	1,215.3	2,896.0
Cincinnati, OH	4.2	175.5	331.3
Cleveland, OH	34.7	198.5	478.4
Colorado Springs, CO	43.3	291.1	360.9
Columbus, OH	17.5	483.3	711.5
Corpus Christi, TX	150.7	198.7	277.5
Dallas, TX	422.6	604.2	1,188.6
Denver, CO	175.7	362.2	554.6
Detroit, MI	47.2	116.6	951.3
El Paso, TX	431.9	413.1	563.7
Fort Worth, TX	159.4	319.2	534.7
Fresno, CA	170.5	214.6	427.7
Honolulu, HI	16.2	73.1	371.7
Houston, TX	730.9	962.6	1,953.6
Indianapolis, IN	30.6	540.2	781.9
Jacksonville, FL	30.6	474.3	735.6
Kansas City, MO	30.6	267.9	441.5
Las Vegas, NV	113.0	334.2	478.4
Lexington-Fayette, KY	8.6	211.1	260.5
Long Beach, CA	165.1	208.4	461.5
Los Angeles, CA	1,719.1	1,734.0	3,694.8
Louisville, KY	4.8	161.3	256.2
Memphis, TN	19.3	223.7	650.1
Mesa, AZ	78.3	323.7	396.4
Miami, FL	238.4	241.5	362.5
Milwaukee, WI	71.6	298.4	597.0

Table 1.10   continued

	Hispanic	White	Total
Minneapolis, MN	29.2	249.2	382.6
Nashville-Davidson, TN	25.8	359.6	545.5
New Orleans, LA	14.8	136.0	484.7
New York, NY	2,160.6	3,576.4	8,008.3
Newark, NJ	80.6	72.5	273.5
Oakland, CA	87.5	125.0	399.5
Oklahoma City, OK	51.4	346.2	506.1
Omaha, NE	29.4	305.7	390.0
Philadelphia, PA	128.9	683.3	1,517.6
Phoenix, AZ	450.0	938.9	1,321.0
Pittsburgh, PA	4.4	226.3	334.6
Portland, OR	36.1	412.2	529.1
Raleigh, NC	19.3	174.8	276.1
Riverside, CA	97.3	151.4	255.2
Sacramento, CA	88.0	196.5	407.0
San Antonio, TX	671.4	774.7	1,144.6
San Diego, CA	310.8	736.2	1,223.4
San Francisco, CA	109.5	385.7	776.7
San Jose, CA	270.0	425.0	894.9
Santa Ana, CA	257.1	144.4	338.0
Seattle, WA	29.7	394.9	563.4
St. Louis, MO	7.0	152.7	348.2
St. Paul, MN	22.7	192.4	287.2
Tampa, FL	58.5	194.9	303.4
Toledo, OH	17.1	220.3	313.6
Tucson, AZ	173.9	341.4	486.7
Tulsa, OK	28.1	275.5	393.0
Virginia Beach, VA	17.8	303.7	425.3
Washington, DC	45.0	176.1	572.1
Wichita, KS	33.1	258.9	344.3

SOURCE: U.S. Bureau of the Census, <u>Statistical Abstract of the United States, 2001</u>,
p. 39, table 36; p. 38, table 35. C 3.134:001

NOTES: As of April. Data refer to boundaries in effect on January 1, 2000.

UNITS: Population in thousands of persons.

Table 1.11   Resident Population, by State, Projections for 2020

	Hispanic	White	Total
Alabama	1.2%	72.0%	5,231
Alaska	4.8	65.2	866
Arizona	31.7	85.0	5,713
Arkansas	1.9	83.1	3,005
California	36.5	71.0	47,953
Colorado	20.0	90.1	4,871
Connecticut	12.9	85.2	3,617
Delaware	5.9	70.7	871
District of Columbia	6.1	33.0	636
Florida	21.5	78.9	19,449
Georgia	3.2	66.9	9,426
Hawaii	13.7	47.9	1,815
Idaho	11.7	95.3	1,600
Illinois	15.7	75.2	13,218
Indiana	4.0	87.7	6,488
Iowa	3.2	94.6	3,038
Kansas	7.9	87.4	3,130
Kentucky	1.0	89.7	4,313
Louisiana	3.6	63.9	5,193
Maine	1.4	97.7	1,400
Maryland	5.0	59.6	6,289
Massachusetts	9.9	86.5	6,363
Michigan	4.6	77.0	10,377
Minnesota	2.8	90.1	5,426
Mississippi	1.0	63.1	3,100
Missouri	2.2	85.5	6,123
Montana	2.6	90.4	1,071
Nebraska	6.5	92.5	1,885
Nevada	26.1	81.3	2,145
New Hampshire	2.2	95.6	1,399
New Jersey	17.0	73.5	9,058
New Mexico	55.4	82.7	2,338

continued on the next page

Table 1.11   continued

	Hispanic	White	Total
New York	15.9%	70.6%	19,111
North Carolina	2.4	72.3	9,014
North Dakota	1.4	90.8	719
Ohio	2.9	83.8	11,870
Oklahoma	5.0	80.0	4,020
Oregon	8.1	89.1	4,367
Pennsylvania	4.9	85.4	12,656
Rhode Island	11.3	88.6	1,090
South Carolina	1.8	66.5	4,685
South Dakota	1.6	83.7	863
Tennessee	1.3	80.6	6,434
Texas	40.3	82.9	25,592
Utah	8.0	90.9	2,749
Vermont	1.5	97.1	658
Virginia	4.7	72.5	8,388
Washington	8.9	84.8	7,960
West Virginia	1.1	95.6	1,852
Wisconsin	4.6	87.8	5,846
Wyoming	8.5	93.9	658

SOURCE: U.S. Bureau of the Census, Statistical Abstract of the United States, 1991; p. 22, table 27 (data from U.S. Bureau of the Census, *Current Population Reports*, Series P-25 and Census Press Release CB91-100). C 3.134:(year) U.S. Bureau of the Census, Population Projections for States, by Age, Sex, Race, and Hispanic Origin: 1993 to 2020, tables 1 and 4. From *Current Population Reports*, P25-1111, downloaded from Census Bureau Bulletin Board. Telnet cenbbs.census.gov.

NOTES: 'Total' includes other races/ethnic groups not shown separately. 1990 data from the 1990 Census, 2000 data from projections by the US Bureau of the Census.

UNITS: Population in thousands of persons.

Chapter 2: Social Characteristics

Table 2.01 Marital Status, Persons 15 Years Old and Older, 1985, 1990, 2000

	Hispanic		White		Total	
	number	percent	number	percent	number	percent
1985						
All marital statuses	11,776	100.0%	157,090	100.0%	182,316	100.0%
single, never married	3,676	31.2	38,177	24.3	47,744	26.2
married, spouse present	6,036	51.3	92,465	58.9	102,229	56.1
married, spouse absent	782	6.6	3,960	2.5	5,770	3.2
widowed	553	4.7	11,404	7.3	13,484	7.4
divorced	729	6.2	11,084	7.1	13,089	7.2
1990						
All marital statuses	14,576	100.0%	163,417	100.0%	191,793	100.0%
single, never married	4,691	32.2	39,516	24.2	50,223	26.2
married, spouse present	7,363	50.5	95,337	58.3	106,513	55.3
married, spouse absent	1,022	7.0	4,191	2.6	6,118	3.2
widowed	548	3.8	11,731	7.2	13,810	7.2
divorced	952	6.5	12,643	7.7	15,128	7.9
2000						
All marital statuses	22,793	100.0%	177,581	100.0%	213,773	100.0%
married, spouse present	11,221	49.2	99,258	55.9	113,002	52.9
married, spouse absent	666	2.9	1,971	1.1	2,730	1.3
widowed	881	3.9	11,532	6.5	13,665	6.4
divorced	1,623	7.1	16,547	9.3	19,881	9.3
separated	845	3.7	2,976	1.7	4,479	2.1
never married	7,558	33.2	45,297	25.5	60,016	28.1

SOURCE: U.S. Bureau of the Census, <u>Current Population Reports: Marital Status and Living Arrangements, March, 1985</u>, Series P-20, #410; p. 17, table 1; <u>March, 1990</u>, #450; p. 17, table 1. c3.186/6:(year); <u>Current Population Reports: America's Families and Living Arrangements, June, 2001</u>, Series P20, #537, table A1. <www.census.gov>

NOTES: 'Total' includes other races and ethnic groups not shown separately.

UNITS: Number in thousands of persons 15 years old and older; percent as a percent of total (percents **not** standardized for age).

Table 2.02   Marital Status, Men 15 Years Old and Older, 1985, 1990, 2000

	Hispanic		White		Total	
	Number	percent	number	percent	number	percent
Men:						
1985						
All marital statuses	5,809	100.0%	75,487	100.0%	87,034	100.0%
single, never married	2,125	36.6	21,276	28.2	26,108	30.0
married, spouse present	2,938	50.6	46,261	61.3	51,114	58.7
married, spouse absent	337	5.8	1,666	2.2	2,439	2.8
widowed	124	2.1	1,744	2.3	2,109	2.4
divorced	285	4.9	4,540	6.0	5,264	6.0
1990						
All marital statuses	7,254	100.0%	78,908	100.0%	91,033	100.0%
single, never married	2,674	36.9	22,078	28.0	27,422	30.1
married, spouse present	3,605	49.7	47,700	60.4	52,924	58.1
married, spouse absent	502	6.9	1,842	2.3	2,360	2.6
widowed	103	1.4	1,930	2.4	2,282	2.5
divorced	370	5.1	5,359	6.8	6,045	6.6
2000						
All marital statuses	11,327	100.0%	86,443	100.0%	103,114	100.0%
married, spouse present	5,550	49.0	49,672	57.5	56,501	54.8
married, spouse absent	402	3.5	979	1.1	1,365	1.3
widowed	170	1.5	2,196	2.5	2,604	2.5
divorced	669	5.9	7,246	8.4	8,572	8.3
separated	288	2.5	1,237	1.4	1,818	1.8
never married	4,249	37.5	25,113	29.1	32,253	31.3

SOURCE: U.S. Bureau of the Census, Current Population Reports: Marital Status and Living Arrangements, March, 1985, Series P-20, #410; p. 17, table 1; March, 1990, #450; p. 17, table 1 C3.186/6:(year); Current Population Reports: America's Families and Living Arrangements, June, 2001, P20-537, table A1. <www.census.gov>

NOTES: 'Total' includes other races and ethnic groups not shown separately.

UNITS: Number in thousands of men 15 years old and older; percent as a percent of total (percents **not** standardized for age).

Table 2.03   Marital Status, Women 15 Years Old and Older, 1985, 1990, 2000

	Hispanic		White		Total	
	Number	percent	number	percent	number	percent
Women:						
1985						
All marital statuses	5,967	100.0%	81,603	100.0%	95,282	100.0%
single, never married	1,551	26.0	16,901	20.7	21,636	22.7
married, spouse present	3,097	51.9	46,205	56.6	51,114	53.6
married, spouse absent	445	7.5	2,294	2.8	3,331	3.5
widowed	430	7.2	9,660	11.8	11,375	11.9
divorced	444	7.4	6,544	8.0	7,826	8.2
1990						
All marital statuses	7,323	100.0%	84,508	100.0%	99,838	100.0%
single, never married	2,017	27.5	17,438	20.6	22,718	22.8
married, spouse present	3,758	51.3	47,637	56.4	53,256	53.3
married, spouse absent	520	7.1	2,349	2.8	3,541	3.5
widowed	445	6.1	9,800	11.6	11,477	11.5
divorced	582	8.0	7,284	8.6	8,845	8.9
2000						
All marital statuses	11,466	100.0%	91,138	100.0%	110,660	100.0%
married, spouse present	5,671	49.5	49,586	54.4	56,501	51.1
married, spouse absent	264	2.3	992	1.1	1,365	1.2
widowed	711	6.2	9,336	10.2	11,061	10.0
divorced	954	8.3	9,301	10.2	11,309	10.2
separated	557	4.9	1,739	1.9	2,661	2.4
never married	3,309	28.9	20,184	22.1	27,763	25.1

SOURCE: U.S. Bureau of the Census, Current Population Reports: Marital Status and Living Arrangements, March, 1985, Series P-20, #410; p. 17, table 1; March, 1990, #450; p. 17, table 1 C3.186/6:(year); Current Population Reports: America's Families and Living Arrangements, June, 2001, P20-537, table A1. <www.census.gov>

NOTES: 'Total' includes other races and ethnic groups not shown separately.

UNITS: Number in thousands of women 15 years old and older; percent as a percent of total (percents **not** standardized for age).

Table 2.04   Marital Status of the Hispanic Population, by Type of Origin, 2000

	Mexican	Puerto Rican	Cuban	Central/ South American	Other Hispanic	Total Hispanic
Total population 15 years old and over						
number	14,547	2,110	1,104	3,551	1,481	22,793
percent	100.0%	100.0%	100.0%	100.0%	100.0%	100.0%
married, spouse present	50.5	42.0	56.1	47.3	46.4	49.2
married, spouse absent	2.8	2.1	1.6	4.3	3.1	2.9
widowed	3.6	3.5	8.7	3.4	4.1	3.9
divorced	6.2	9.6	11.1	6.9	10.2	7.1
separated	3.4	5.0	2.2	4.4	4.5	3.7
never married	33.5	37.8	20.4	33.7	31.7	33.2

SOURCE: U.S. Bureau of the Census, "Current Population Reports: The Hispanic Population of the United States, 2000, (Table) 2.1. Population Age 15 Years and Over by Marital Status, Sex, Hispanic Origin and Race" <http://census.census.gov/population/socdemo/hispanic/p20-535/tab02-1.txt>

NOTES: Total population includes other races and ethnic groups not shown separately. 'Other Hispanic origin' includes persons from Spain and persons identifying themselves generally as Hispanic, Spanish, Spanish-American, Hispano, Latino, etc.

UNITS: Total resident population in thousands of persons 15 years old and over; percent as a percent of total shown (100.0%).

Table 2.05 Characteristics of Unmarried and Married Male-Female Couples: March 2000

	Unmarried couples	Married Couples
both Hispanic	332	4,739
neither Hispanic	3,268	50,015
one Hispanic and one non-Hispanic	222	1,743

SOURCE: U.S. Bureau of the Census, <u>Current Population Reports: America's Families and Living Arrangements, June, 2001</u> Series P20, #537; p. 15, table 8.
<www.census.gov>

UNITS: Thousands of couples.

Table 2.06 Hispanic Married Couple Households, by Type of Origin of the Husband and Wife, 1993

	Mexican	Puerto Rican	Cuban	origin of the wife Central/ South Amer	other Hispanic	total Hispanic
By origin of the wife:						
Total population	100.0%	100.0%	100.0%	100.0%	100.0%	100.0%
total Hispanic population	85.1	81.4	82.9	84.4	65.7	83.1
by origin						
Mexican origin	82.8	2.7	1.7	4.3	1.4	53.6
Puerto Rican origin	0.1	70.7	2.1	2.1	1.4	6.7
Cuban origin	0.1	1.2	77.1	2.8	0.7	5.5
Central/South American origin	1.6	3.7	1.3	74.8	2.1	12.1
other Hispanic origin	0.5	3.0	0.8	0.4	60.1	5.2
not of Hispanic origin	14.9	18.6	17.1	15.6	34.3	16.9
By origin of the husband:						
Total population	4.5%	0.6%	0.4%	1.0%	0.5%	7.1%
total Hispanic population	55.7	7.3	5.4	12.3	5.1	85.8
by origin						
Mexican origin	85.6	0.4	0.2	1.0	0.2	87.3
Puerto Rican origin	0.9	69.3	1.5	3.3	1.2	76.1
Cuban origin	1.3	1.7	79.7	6.5	0.9	90.1
Central/South American origin	7.4	2.3	0.6	77.4	1.2	88.9
other Hispanic origin	4.2	3.8	0.8	0.8	64.9	74.4
not of Hispanic origin	0.7	0.1	0.1	0.2	0.2	1.3

SOURCE: U.S. Bureau of the Census, The Hispanic Population in the United States: March, 1993; p. 6, table A (data from U.S. Bureau of the Census, *Current Population Reports*). C 3.186/14-2:993

NOTES: Total population includes other races and ethnic groups not shown separately. 'Other Hispanic origin' includes persons from Spain and persons identifying themselves generally as Hispanic, Spanish, Spanish-American, Hispano, Latino, etc.

UNITS: Percent as a percent of total shown (100.0%).

Table 2.07   Age, Educational Attainment, and Residence, 1985

	Hispanic	White	Total
Age			
Persons of all ages	16,940	199,117	234,066
persons:			
under 5 years old	1,809	14,610	17,958
5-14 years old	3,355	27,417	33,792
15-44 years old	8,540	93,852	110,948
45-64 years old	2,407	39,033	44,549
65 years old and over	819	24,205	26,818
Years of school completed			
All persons 25 years old and over	8,455	124,905	143,524
persons completing:			
0-8 years of school	3,192	16,224	19,893
1-3 years high school	1,210	14,365	17,553
4 years high school	2,402	48,728	54,866
1-3 years college	932	20,652	23,405
4 or more years college	718	24,935	27,808
Residence			
Northeast	3,144	43,185	49,276
Midwest	1,389	52,280	58,587
South	5,288	63,155	79,165
West	6,964	40,394	46,489
nonfarm	na	na	na
farm	na	na	na
inside metro areas	na	na	na
outside metro areas	na	na	na

SOURCE: U.S. Bureau of the Census, Statistical Abstract of the United States, 1987, p. 35, table 39, (data from U.S. Bureau of the Census, *Current Population Reports*, Series P-25). C 3.134:987
U.S. Bureau of the Census, Current Population Reports: Money Income of Households, Families and Persons in the United States, 1984, Series P-60 (#151), pp. 10-17, table 4. C3.186/22:984

NOTES: 'Total' includes other races and ethnic groups not shown separately.

UNITS: Population in thousands of persons; percent distribution as a percent of total, 100.0%.

Table 2.08 Age, Educational Attainment, and Residence, 1990

	Hispanic	White	Total
Age			
Persons of all ages			
persons:	21,405	208,611	248,644
under 18 years old	7,457	51,929	65,049
18-24 years old	2,741	20,383	24,901
25-44 years old	7,139	68,807	81,570
45-64 years old	2,977	40,594	47,032
65 years old and over	1,091	26,898	30,093
Years of school completed			
All persons 25 years old			
and over	11,208	136,299	158,694
persons that:			
did not complete high school	5,455	27,409	34,228
completed high school,			
no college	3,285	53,250	61,272
completed some college, not			
a college graduate	1,379	25,358	29,169
completed college	1,088	30,283	34,025
Residence			
Northeast	3,531	43,727	50,799
Midwest	1,399	52,771	59,914
South	6,598	66,492	85,097
West	9,878	45,622	52,835
nonfarm	21,297	204,001	243,865
farm	108	4,610	4,779
inside metro areas	19,883	159,443	193,052
outside metro areas	1,522	49,168	55,592

SOURCE: U.S. Bureau of the Census, Current Population Reports: Poverty in the United States: 1990, Series P-60, #175; p. 24, table 5; pp. 84-87, table 11; p. 154, table 21. C3.186/11:990

NOTES: 'Total' includes other races and ethnic groups not shown separately.

UNITS: Population in thousands of persons; percent distribution as a percent of total, 100.0%.

Table 2.09   Age and Residence, 2000

	Hispanic	White	Total
Age			
Persons of all ages			
persons:	33,716	225,997	275,924
under 18 years old	11,884	56,412	71,936
18-24 years old	4,178	21,532	26,965
25-34 years old	5,641	29,867	37,440
35-44 years old	5,037	36,691	44,780
45-54 years old	3,212	31,964	38,040
55-59 years old	1,052	11,450	13,338
60-64 years old	831	8,960	10,447
65 years old and over	1,882	29,122	32,978
Residence			
Northeast	4,556	43,604	52,228
Midwest	2,577	55,055	63,586
South	11,768	74,630	96,759
West	14,816	52,708	63,351
inside metro areas	30,959	180,296	224,349
outside metro areas	2,757	45,701	51,575

SOURCE: U.S. Bureau of the Census, "Current Population Reports: Poverty in the United States, (Table) 2. Age, Sex, Household Relationship, Race and Hispanic Origin by Ratio of Income to Poverty Level: 2000;" <http://ferret.bls.census.gov/macro/032001/pov/new02_000.htm>; (accessed: 21 March 2002); "(Table) 19. Region, Division, and Type of Residence – Poverty Status of Families and People in 2000," <http://ferret.bls.census.gov/macro/032001/pov/new19_007.htm>; (accessed: 21 March 2002)

NOTES: 'Total' includes other races and ethnic groups not shown separately.

UNITS: Population in thousands of persons.

Chapter 3:
Household & Family Characteristics

Table 3.01 Selected Characteristics of Households, 1985

	Hispanic	White	Total
Marital status and sex of the householder			
All households, both sexes	4,883	75,328	86,789
male householder	3,357	53,868	60,025
married, wife present	2,638	43,444	47,683
married, wife absent	129	1,013	1,416
widowed	84	1,386	1,620
divorced	162	3,078	3,535
single, never married	344	4,947	5,772
female householder	1,526	21,461	26,763
married, husband present	186	2,199	2,667
married, husband absent	351	1,668	2,497
widowed	313	8,304	9,728
divorced	334	5,203	6,265
single, never married	342	4,087	5,606
Age of the householder			
All ages	4,883	75,328	86,789
15-24 years old	489	4,626	5,438
25-34 years old	1,363	17,010	20,013
35-44 years old	1,184	15,024	17,481
45-54 years old	743	10,792	12,628
55-64 years old	606	11,471	13,073
65 years old and over	497	16,406	18,155
Housing tenure			
All tenures	4,883	75,328	86,789
own housing unit	2,007	50,611	55,845
rent housing unit	2,876	24,667	30,943

continued on the next page

Table 3.01   continued

	Hispanic	White	Total
Size of the household			
All household sizes	4,883	75,328	86,789
one person	756	17,876	20,602
two persons	1,026	24,558	27,289
three persons	995	13,336	15,465
four persons	959	11,795	13,631
five persons	576	5,061	6,108
six persons	297	1,819	2,299
seven or more persons	275	882	1,296
persons per household	2.96	2.64	2.69
Residence			
All residences	4,883	75,328	86,789
Northeast	1,017	16,244	18,348
Midwest	376	19,599	21,697
South	1,553	24,283	29,581
West	1,937	15,202	17,163
inside metropolitan areas	na	na	na
outside metropolitan areas	na	na	na
nonfarm	na	na	na
farm	na	na	na

SOURCE: U.S. Bureau of the Census, <u>Current Population Reports: Money Income of Households Families and Persons in the United States; March 1984</u>, Series P-60, #151, pp. 10-14, table 4. C3.186/2:984

U.S. Bureau of the Census, <u>Current Population Reports: Household & Family Characteristics, March 1985</u>, Series P-20, #411, pp. 107-112, table 22. C3.186/17:985

NOTES: 'Total' includes other races and ethnic groups not shown separately.

UNITS: Number of households in thousands of households; persons per household, average.

Table 3.02   Selected Characteristics of Households, 1990

	Hispanic	White	Total
Marital status and sex of the householder			
All households, both sexes	5,933	80,163	93,347
family households	4,840	56,590	66,090
married couple families	3,395	46,981	52,317
male householder, no wife present	329	2,303	2,884
female householder, no husband present	1,116	7,306	10,890
non-family households	1,093	23,573	27,257
male householder	587	9,951	11,606
-living alone	415	7,718	9,049
female householder	506	13,622	15,651
-living alone	442	12,161	13,950
Age of the householder			
All ages	5,933	80,163	93,347
15-24 years old	542	4,222	5,121
25-34 years old	1,721	17,137	20,472
35-44 years old	1,405	17,395	20,554
45-54 years old	930	12,404	14,514
55-64 years old	664	10,862	12,529
65 years old and over	671	18,144	20,156
Housing tenure			
All tenures	5,933	80,163	93,347
own housing unit	2,443	54,094	59,846
rent housing unit	3,383	24,685	31,895

continued on the next page

Table 3.02   continued

	Hispanic	White	Total
Size of the household			
All household sizes	5,933	80,163	93,347
one person	856	19,879	22,999
two persons	1,292	26,714	30,114
three persons	1,139	13,585	16,128
four persons	1,172	12,399	14,456
five persons	752	5,104	6,213
six persons	386	1,615	2,143
seven or more persons	336	877	1,295
persons per household	3.48	2.58	2.63
Residence			
All residences	5,933	80,163	93,347
Northeast	1,037	16,773	19,127
Midwest	398	20,339	22,760
South	1,953	26,155	32,262
West	2,544	16,896	19,197
inside metropolitan areas	5,479	61,155	72,331
outside metropolitan areas	454	19,009	21,016
nonfarm	8,897	78,556	91,710
farm	36	1,608	1,637

SOURCE: U.S. Bureau of the Census, Current Population Reports: Money Income of Households Families and Persons in the United States: 1988 and 1989, Series P-60, #172, pp. 9-12, table 1. C3.186/2:989

NOTES: 'Total' includes other races and ethnic groups not shown separately.

UNITS: Number of households in thousands of households; persons per household, average.

Table 3.03   Selected Characteristics of Households, 2000

	Hispanic	White	Total
Marital status and type of householder			
All households, both sexes	9,663	88,545	106,417
family households	7,728	60,211	72,375
married couple families	5,246	48,644	55,598
male householder, no wife present	736	3,274	4,252
female householder, no husband present	1,745	8,293	12,525
non-family households	1,935	28,334	34,042
male householder	1,024	12,582	15,218
-living alone	667	9,489	11,537
female householder	911	15,752	18,824
-living alone	736	13,685	16,286
Age of the householder			
All ages	9,663	88,545	106,417
15-24 years old	970	4,956	6,392
25-34 years old	2,500	14,653	18,554
35-44 years old	2,479	19,472	23,904
45-54 years old	1,636	18,169	21,797
55-64 years old	1,006	11,902	13,943
65 years old and over	1,072	19,393	21,828

continued on the next page

Table 3.03 continued

	Hispanic	White	Total
Size of the household			
All household sizes	9,663	88,545	106,417
one person	1,403	23,174	27,823
two persons	2,056	30,373	35,389
three persons	1,813	13,855	17,260
four persons	1,986	12,724	15,428
five persons	1,248	5,465	6,683
six persons	670	1,845	2,396
seven or more persons	487	1,109	1,439
Residence			
All residences	9,663	88,545	106,417
Northeast	1,470	17,172	20,212
Midwest	697	21,471	24,497
South	3,528	30,224	38,525
West	3,968	19,677	23,183
inside metropolitan areas	8,854	69,972	85,737
outside metropolitan areas	808	18,572	20,681

SOURCE: U.S. Bureau of the Census, "Current Population Reports: Income 2000, (Table) 1. Median Income of Households by Selected Characteristics, Race, and Hispanic Origin of Householder: 2000, 1999, and 1998;" published 20 September 2001; <http://www.census.gov/hhes/income/income00/inctab1.html>

NOTES: 'Total' includes other races and ethnic groups not shown separately.

UNITS: Number of households in thousands of households.

Table 3.04   Type and Tenure of Hispanic Households, by Type of Hispanic Origin, 2000

	Mexican	Puerto Rican	Cuban	Central/ South American	Other Hispanic	Total Hispanic
Households						
Total	5,733	1,004	523	1,372	687	9,319
Family households	4,794	770	385	1,109	504	7,561
Percent by tenure						
owner occupied	47.8%	35.0%	58.7%	37.6%	48.0%	45.5%
renter occupied	52.2	65.0	41.3	62.4	52.0	54.5

SOURCE: U.S. Bureau of the Census, "Current Population Reports: The Hispanic Population of the United States, 2000, (Table) 3.1. Household Type by Hispanic Origin and Race of Householder: March 2000"; "Current Population Reports: The Hispanic Population of the United States, 2000, (Table) 16.1. Household Tenure by Household Type, and by Hispanic Origin and Race of Householder: March 2000" published March 6, 2001. <http://www..census.gov/population/socdemo/Hispanic/p20-535/tab03-1.txt>, <http://www..census.gov/population/socdemo/Hispanic/p20-535/tab16-1.txt>

NOTES: Total population includes other races and ethnic groups not shown separately. 'Other Hispanic origin' includes persons from Spain and persons identifying themselves generally as Hispanic, Spanish, Spanish-American, Hispano, Latino, etc.

UNITS: Households in thousands of households; percent as a percent of all households by type (100.0%).

Table 3.05   Selected Characteristics of Family Households, 1985

	Hispanic	White	Total
Type of family			
All families	3,939	54,400	62,706
married couple families	2,824	45,643	50,350
male householder,			
no wife present	210	1,816	2,228
female householder,			
no husband present	905	6,941	10,129
Size of family			
All family sizes	3,939	54,400	62,706
two persons	962	22,711	25,349
three persons	948	12,743	14,804
four persons	936	11,517	13,259
five persons	552	4,894	5,894
six persons	276	1,704	2,175
seven or more persons	266	831	1,225
average per family	3.88	3.16	3.23
Number of related children			
under 18 years old			
All families	3,939	54,400	62,706
no children	1,337	28,169	31,594
one child	904	11,174	13,108
two children	865	9,937	11,645
three children	481	3,695	4,486
four children	215	1,049	1,329
five children	87	261	373
six or more children	50	115	171
average per family	1.44	0.88	0.92
average per family			
with children	2.18	1.83	1.85

continued on the next page

Table 3.05   continued

	Hispanic	White	Total
Number of earners			
All families	3,905	53,777	61,930
no earner	599	7,674	9,221
one earner	1,290	15,219	17,949
two earners	1,485	23,303	26,160
three earners	370	5,317	6,029
four earners or more	161	2,263	2,570
Housing tenure			
All tenures	3,939	54,400	62,706
own housing unit	1,772	40,865	45,015
rent housing unit	2,167	13,535	17,691
Residence			
All residences	3,939	54,400	62,706
Northeast	808	11,631	13,149
Midwest	313	14,309	15,839
South	1,273	17,953	21,781
West	1,545	10,507	11,938
nonfarm	na	na	na
farm	na	na	na
inside metropolitan areas	na	na	na
outside metropolitan areas	na	na	na

SOURCE: U.S. Bureau of the Census, Current Population Reports: Money Income of
Households, Families, and Persons in the United States, 1984, Series P-
60, #151, pp. 76-77, table 21. C3.186/2:984
U.S. Bureau of the Census, Current Population Reports: Household &
Family Characteristics, March 1985, Series P-20, #437, pp. 13-45, table
1; pp. 107-111, table 22. C3.186/17:985

NOTES: 'Total' includes other races and ethnic groups not shown separately.
'Number of earners' excludes families with members in the armed
forces.

UNITS: Number of households in thousands of family households.

Table 3.06   Selected Characteristics of Family Households, 1990

	Hispanic	White	Total
Type of family			
All families	4,840	56,590	66,090
married couple families	3,395	46,981	52,317
male householder, no			
wife present	329	2,303	2,884
female householder, no			
husband present	1,116	7,306	10,890
Size of family			
All family sizes	4,840	56,590	66,090
two persons	1,226	24,438	27,606
three persons	1,114	12,937	15,353
four persons	1,146	12,048	14,036
five persons	714	4,882	5,938
six persons	347	1,505	1,997
seven or more persons	293	781	1,170
average per family	3.83	3.11	3.17
Number of related children			
under 18 years old			
All families	4,840	56,590	66,090
no children	1,790	29,872	33,801
one child	1,095	11,186	13,530
two children	1,036	10,342	12,263
three children	579	3,853	4,650
four children	232	970	1,279
five children	73	247	379
six or more children	35	121	188
average per family	1.34	0.86	0.89
average per family			
with children	2.12	1.82	1.83

continued on the next page

Table 3.06   continued

	Hispanic	White	Total
Number of earners			
All families	4,840	56,590	66,090
no earner	615	7,816	9,439
one earner	1,554	14,970	18,146
two earners	1,860	25,737	29,235
three earners	541	5,832	6,724
four earners or more	271	2,236	2,546
Housing tenure			
All tenures	4,840	56,590	66,090
own housing unit	3,448	42,588	47,142
rent housing unit	2,678	14,003	18,948
Residence			
All residences	4,840	56,590	66,090
Northeast	815	11,837	13,494
Midwest	330	14,370	16,059
South	1,596	18,746	23,244
West	2,101	11,638	13,293
nonfarm	4,813	55,225	64,701
farm	28	1,365	1,390
inside metropolitan areas	6,256	42,592	50,619
outside metropolitan areas	1,215	13,999	15,471

SOURCE: U.S. Bureau of the Census, Current Population Reports: Money Income of
              Households, Families, and Persons in the United States: 1988 and 1989,
              Series P-60, #172, pp. 9-11, table 1; pp. 48-50, table 13; pp. 76-80,
              table 18. C3.186/2:989
              U.S. Bureau of the Census, Current Population Reports: Household &
              Family Characteristics: March 1990 and 1989, Series P-20, #447, pp. 13-
              16, table 1; pp. 18-20, table 2. C3.186/17:989

NOTES: 'Total' includes other races and ethnic groups not shown separately.
              'Number of earners' excludes families with members in the armed
              forces.

UNITS: Number of households in thousands of family households.

Table 3.07   Selected Characteristics of Family Households, 2000

	Hispanic	White	Total
Type of family			
All families	7,728	60,218	72,383
married couple families	5,246	48,651	55,606
male householder, no			
wife present	736	3,274	4,252
female householder, no			
husband present	1,745	8,293	12,526
Size of family			
All family sizes	7,728	60,218	72,383
two persons	1,938	27,457	31,957
three persons	1,745	12,895	16,080
four persons	1,869	12,096	14,636
five persons	1,164	5,123	6,256
six persons	598	1,684	2,192
seven or more persons	414	963	1,263

continued on the next page

Table 3.07   continued

	Hispanic	White	Total
Number of earners			
All families	7,728	60,218	72,383
no earner	688	7,944	9,384
one earner	2,652	17,084	21,713
two earners	3,126	27,683	32,399
three earners	880	5,517	6,600
four earners or more	381	1,989	2,287
Residence			
All residences	7,728	60,218	72,383
Northeast	1,101	11,393	13,420
Midwest	573	14,606	16,645
South	2,814	21,022	26,602
West	3,239	13,198	15,717
inside metropolitan areas	7,077	47,209	57,896
outside metropolitan areas	651	13,009	14,487

SOURCE: U.S. Bureau of the Census, "Current Population Reports: Income 2000, (Table) 4. Median Income of Families by Selected Characteristics, Race, and Hispanic Origin of Householder: 2000, 1999, and 1998;" published 20 September 2001; <http://www.census.gov/hhes/income/income00/inctab4.html>

NOTES: 'Total' includes other races and ethnic groups not shown separately. 'Number of earners' excludes families with members in the armed forces.

UNITS: Number of households in thousands of family households.

Table 3.08   Type and Size of Hispanic Family Households, by Type of Hispanic Origin, 2000

	Mexican	Puerto Rican	Cuban	Central/ South American	Other Hispanic	Total Hispanic
All family households	100.0%	100.0%	100.0%	100.0%	100.0%	100.0%
married couple families	69.9	56.8	77.1	65.0	64.7	67.9
male householder	8.9	7.4	4.6	10.4	7.9	8.7
female householder	21.1	35.8	18.3	24.6	27.4	23.4
two persons	18.7	29.5	41.3	20.2	27.1	21.7
three persons	21.2	26.1	19.1	25.5	26.2	22.6
four persons	24.6	26.3	25.5	26.3	25.3	25.1
five persons	17.8	11.7	9.6	17.7	13.8	16.5
six persons	9.0	3.0	3.4	5.4	4.2	7.3
seven or more persons	8.7	3.4	1.1	4.9	3.5	6.9

Source: U.S. Bureau of the Census, "Current Population Reports: The Hispanic Population of the United States, 2000, (Table) 4.1.Family and Nonfamily Household Type by Hispanic Origin and Race of Householder: March 2000," published March 6, 2001.
<http: //www..census.gov/population/socdemo/Hispanic/p20-535/tab04-1.txt>
U.S. Bureau of the Census, "Current Population Reports: The Hispanic Population of the United States, 2000, (Table) 5.1. Household Type and Size and by Hispanic Origin and Race of Householder: March 2000," published March 6, 2001.
<http: //www..census.gov/population/socdemo/Hispanic/p20-535/tab05-1.txt>

NOTES: Total population includes other races and ethnic groups not shown separately. 'Other Hispanic origin' includes persons from Spain and persons identifying themselves generally as Hispanic, Spanish, Spanish-American, Hispano, Latino, etc.

UNITS: Family households by type as a percent of all households as shown (100.0%).

Table 3.09 Single Parents Living With Own Children Under 18 Years Old, 2000

	Hispanic	White	Total
Single Fathers			
With own children under 18	313	1,622	2,044
With own children under 12	260	1,145	1,441
With own children under 6	189	647	819
With own children under 3	129	393	511
With own children under 1	51	152	196
Single Mothers			
With own children under 18	1,565	6,216	9,681
With own children under 12	1,190	4,558	7,337
With own children under 6	720	2,519	4,115
With own children under 3	409	1,396	2,319
With own children under 1	141	499	824

SOURCE: U.S. Bureau of the Census, Current Population Reports: America's Families and Living Arrangements, June 2001, Series P-20, #537; p. 8, table 4.
<www.census.gov>

NOTES: 'Total' includes other races and ethnic groups not shown separately.

UNITS: Thousands of fathers or mothers.

Table 3.10   Living Arrangements of Children Under 18 Years of Age, 2000

	Hispanic children	White children	All children
Living with both parents	7,561	42,497	49,795
Living with mother only	2,919	9,765	16,162
Living with father only	506	2,427	3,058
Living with neither parent	626	1,752	2,981

SOURCE: U.S. Bureau of the Census, <u>Current Population Reports: America's Families and Living Arrangements: June, 2001</u> Series P-20, #537, pp. 1, 25, 37, 60, table C2. <www.census.gov>

NOTES: 'All children' includes children of other races and ethnic groups not shown separately.

UNITS: Thousands of children.

Table 3.11   Primary Child Care Arrangements Used for Preschoolers
by Families With Employed Mothers, Fall 1995

	Hispanic children	White children	All children
All preschoolers with employed mothers	1,002	7,359	10,047
Mother while working	3.8%	6.6%	5.9%
Father	20.1	19.1	18.2
Sibling	1.3	1.0	1.3
Grandparent	18.0	16.7	17.4
Other relative	7.9	3.3	4.7
Daycare center	17.4	18.9	19.4
Nursery/preschool	4.0	6.9	6.5
Head start	1.1	0.9	1.6
Family day care	10.7	17.7	17.2
Other non-relative	15.8	13.9	14.0
Self care	0.0	0.1	0.1

SOURCE: U.S. Bureau of the Census, Current Population Reports: Who's Minding our
Preschoolers? Fall 1995 (Update) Series P70-70, table 4B. C3.186/P70-70

NOTES: 'All children' includes children of other races not shown separately.
Because of multiple arrangements, numbers and percentages may exceed
the total number of children.

UNITS: Thousands of children living in family households.

Chapter 4: Education - Preprimary through High School

Table 4.01   School Enrollment by Age, 2000

	enrollment			enrollment rate		
	Hispanic	White	Total	Hispanic	White	Total
all persons 3 years and over	10,163	46,660	72,214	32.6%	25.0%	27.5%
persons 3 and 4 years old	518	2,607	4,097	35.9	54.6	52.1
persons 5 and 6 years old	1,390	4,639	7,648	94.3	95.5	95.6
persons 7 to 9 years old	1,936	7,576	12,083	97.5	98.4	98.1
persons 10 and 13 years old	2,437	10,305	16,213	97.4	98.5	98.3
persons 14 and 15 years old	1,093	5,135	7,885	96.2	98.9	98.7
persons 16 and 17 years old	959	4,933	7,341	87.0	94.0	92.8
persons 18 and 19 years old	617	3,337	4,926	49.5	63.9	61.2
persons 20 and 21 years old	311	2,388	3,314	26.1	49.2	44.1
persons 22 to 24 years old	309	1,809	2,731	18.2	24.9	24.6
persons 25 to 29 years old	198	1,286	2,030	7.4	11.1	11.4
persons 30 to 34 years old	160	785	1,292	5.6	6.1	6.7
persons 35 to 44 years old	173	1,092	1,632	3.4	3.4	3.7
persons 45 to 54 years old	48	622	810	1.6	2.2	2.2
persons 55 years old and over	14	147	211	0.4	0.3	0.4

SOURCE: U.S. Bureau of the Census, "Current Population Reports: School Enrollment, (Table) 1. Enrollment Status of the Population 3 Years Old and Over, by Age, Sex, Race, Hispanic 1 Origin, Nativity, and Selected Educational Characteristics: October 2000;' published 1 June 2001, <http://www.census.gov/population/socdemo/school/ppl-148/tab01.txt>

NOTES: 'Total' includes other races and ethnic groups not shown separately. 'White' does not include 'Hispanic'.

UNITS: Enrollment in thousands of persons enrolled. All years: rate as a percent of the civilian non-institutionalized population, by age group.

Table 4.02   School Enrollment by Level and Control of School, 2000

	Hispanic	White	Total
Total enrolled	8,647	35,928	56,639
public	8,137	29,882	48,977
private	510	6,046	7,661
nursery school	574	2,854	4,401
public	419	1,149	2,217
private	154	1,705	2,184
kindergarten	687	2,346	3,832
public	639	1,846	3,173
private	48	500	659
elementary school	5,213	20,567	32,867
public	5,000	17,740	29,347
private	213	2,827	3,520
high school	2,174	10,161	15,539
public	2,080	9,147	14,240
private	95	1,013	1,299

SOURCE: U.S. Bureau of the Census, "Current Population Reports: School Enrollment, (Table) 5. Level of Enrollment Below College for People 3 to 24 Years Old, By Control of School, Sex, Metropolitan Status, Race and Hispanic Origin: October 2000;' published 1 June 2001, <http://www.census.gov/population/socdemo/school/ppl-148/tab05.txt>

NOTES: 'Total' includes other races and ethnic groups not shown separately. 'White' does not include 'Hispanic'.

UNITS: Enrollment in thousands of persons enrolled; civilian non-institutionalized population.

Table 4.03   Estimates of the School Age Population, by Age and
Sex, 2000

	Hispanic	White	Total
Both sexes			
3 years old and over	31,158	186,282	263,053
3 and 4 years old	1,444	4,773	7,869
5 and 6 years old	1,474	4,860	8,002
7 to 9 years old	1,985	7,703	12,320
10-13 years old	2,501	10,459	16,492
14 and 15 years old	1,136	5,193	7,993
16 and 17 years old	1,103	5,247	7,910
18 and 19 years old	1,248	5,221	8,045
20 and 21 years old	1,191	4,852	7,508
22 to 24 years old	1,696	7,254	11,105
25 to 29 years old	2,692	11,563	17,782
30 to 34 years old	2,875	12,934	19,429
35 to 44 years old	5,098	31,770	44,684
45 to 54 years old	2,985	28,576	37,312
55 years old and over	3,731	45,878	56,604
Male			
3 years old and over	15,509	91,131	128,044
3 and 4 years old	730	2,454	4,007
5 and 6 years old	768	2,468	4,105
7 to 9 years old	958	3,996	6,304
10-13 years old	1,306	5,331	8,449
14 and 15 years old	576	2,670	4,103
16 and 17 years old	553	2,719	4,064
18 and 19 years old	656	2,628	4,037
20 and 21 years old	613	2,477	3,777
22 to 24 years old	902	3,565	5,525
25 to 29 years old	1,310	5,752	8,566
30 to 34 years old	1,444	6,402	9,547
35 to 44 years old	2,562	15,844	22,021
45 to 54 years old	1,493	14,093	18,238
55 years old and over	1,637	20,732	25,300

continued on the next page

Table 4.03   continued

	Hispanic	White	Total
Female			
3 years old and over	15,649	95,152	135,010
3 and 4 years old	713	2,319	3,863
5 and 6 years old	705	2,392	3,897
7 to 9 years old	1,027	3,707	6,016
10-13 years old	1,195	5,128	8,042
14 and 15 years old	561	2,523	3,889
16 and 17 years old	550	2,528	3,847
18 and 19 years old	591	2,593	4,008
20 and 21 years old	578	2,375	3,731
22 to 24 years old	794	3,689	5,580
25 to 29 years old	1,382	5,812	9,215
30 to 34 years old	1,430	6,533	9,882
35 to 44 years old	2,536	15,926	22,663
45 to 54 years old	1,492	14,483	19,073
55 years old and over	2,094	25,145	31,304

SOURCE: U.S. Bureau of the Census, "Current Population Reports: School Enrollment, (Table) 1. Enrollment Status of the Population 3 Years Old and Over, by Age, Sex, Race, Hispanic 1 Origin, Nativity, and Selected Educational Characteristics: October 2000;' published 1 June 2001, <http://www.census.gov/population/socdemo/school/ppl-148/tab01.txt>

NOTES: 'Total' includes other races and ethnic groups not shown separately. 'White' does not include 'Hispanic'.

UNITS: Estimates of the civilian non-institutionalized population, 3-years old and over as of October 1, in thousands of persons.

Table 4.04 Preprimary School Enrollment of Children 3 - 5 Years Old, by Selected Characteristic of the Mother, 1998

	Hispanic	White	Total
All children 3 and 4 years old			
enrolled in nursery school	450	2,442	3,762
mother employed part-time	60	495	686
mother employed full-time	162	986	1,546
mother unemployed	14	35	109
mother with 0-8 years of school	94	9	121
with mother high school graduate	128	557	912
with mother with bachelor's degree or more	28	952	1,169
All children 3 and 4 years old			
enrolled in kindergarten	69	164	335
mother employed part-time	7	46	61
mother employed full-time	24	68	150
mother unemployed	-	6	6
mother with 0-8 years of school	10	na	10
with mother high school graduate	19	30	75
with mother with bachelor's degree or more	7	50	83

continued on the next page

Table 4.04   continued

	Hispanic	White	Total
All children 5 years old enrolled in nursery school	96	371	565
mother employed part-time	20	75	103
mother employed full-time	45	160	254
mother unemployed	na	7	10
mother with 0-8 years of school	14	14	
with mother high school graduate	31	80	128
with mother with bachelor's degree or more	15	137	164
All children 5 years old enrolled in kindergarten	541	1,793	2,931
mother employed part-time	42	374	461
mother employed full-time	198	705	1,200
mother unemployed	34	30	81
mother with 0-8 years of school	92	10	113
with mother high school graduate	142	456	779
with mother with bachelor's degree or more	28	608	709

SOURCE: U.S. Bureau of the Census, "Current Population Reports: School Enrollment, (Table) 4. Preprimary School Enrollment of People 3 to 6 Years Old, by Control of School, Mother's Labor Force Status and Education, Family Income, Race, and Hispanic Origin: October 2000;' published 1 June 2001, <http://www.census.gov/population/socdemo/school/ppl-148/tab04.txt>

NOTES: 'Total' includes other races/ethnic groups not shown separately. Includes children enrolled in public and non-public nursery school and kindergarten programs. Excludes five year olds enrolled in elementary school. 'All children' includes children whose mothers' labor force status is unknown and children with no mother present in the household. 'White' does not include 'Hispanic'.

UNITS: Enrollment in thousands of children enrolled.

Table 4.05 Enrollment in Public Elementary and Secondary Schools, by
State, Fall, 1998

	Hispanic	White	Total
Alabama	0.9%	61.5%	100.0%
Alaska	3.0	62.5	"
Arizona	31.7	55.5	"
Arkansas	2.5	72.8	"
California	41.4	37.9	"
Colorado	19.9	70.6	"
Connecticut	12.4	71.2	"
Delaware	4.9	62.4	"
District of Columbia	8.3	4.3	"
Florida	17.2	55.3	"
Georgia	3.4	56.4	"
Hawaii	4.6	20.8	"
Idaho	9.7	87.1	"
Illinois	13.9	61.4	"
Indiana	2.8	84.7	"
Iowa	2.8	91.4	"
Kansas	7.5	80.6	"
Kentucky	0.7	88.4	"
Louisiana	1.3	49.7	"
Maine	0.5	97.0	"
Maryland	4.0	55.0	"
Massachusetts	10.0	77.1	"
Michigan	3.0	74.7	"
Minnesota	2.5	85.6	"
Mississippi	0.5	47.7	"
Missouri	1.4	80.2	"
Montana	1.6	86.8	"
Nebraska	5.9	84.8	"
Nevada	22.0	61.2	"
New Hampshire	1.4	96.2	"
New Jersey	14.3	61.6	"

continued on the next page

Table 4.05   continued

	Hispanic	White	Total
New Mexico	48.8%	37.2%	100.0%
New York	18.1	55.6	"
North Carolina	3.1	62.5	"
North Dakota	1.2	89.9	"
Ohio	1.5	81.5	"
Oklahoma	4.9	67.0	"
Oregon	8.7	82.9	"
Pennsylvania	4.0	79.4	"
Rhode Island	12.3	76.4	"
South Carolina	1.2	55.7	"
South Dakota	1.0	87.5	"
Tennessee	1.2	73.6	"
Texas	38.6	44.1	"
Utah	7.2	87.9	"
Vermont	0.4	97.1	"
Virginia	3.9	64.9	"
Washington	9.1	76.1	"
West Virginia	0.5	94.9	"
Wisconsin	3.8	81.9	"
Wyoming	6.7	88.6	"

SOURCE: U.S. Department of Education, National Center for Education Statistics, *Digest of Education Statistics, 2000*; p. 58, table 44. ED 1.113\000

NOTES: 'Total' includes other races and ethnic groups not shown separately. 'White' excludes persons of Hispanic origin.

UNITS: Enrollment as a percent of total enrollment, 100.0%.

Table 4.06 Public Elementary and Secondary School Teachers, by
Selected Characteristic, 1993-94

	Hispanic	White	Total
Total number of teachers	108,744	2,216,605	2,561,294
Percent of teachers, by **highest degree earned**			
no degree	0.9%	0.5%	0.6%
associate degree	0.5	0.1	0.2
bachelor's degree	62.8	51.8	52.0
master's degree	29.8	42.5	42.0
education specialist	4.6	4.4	4.6
doctor's	1.4	0.7	0.7
Percent of teachers, by **years of full-time teaching** **experience**			
less than 3 years	16.7%	9.4%	9.7%
3-9 years	32.1	25.5	25.5
10-20 years	34.1	35.2	35.0
over 20 years	17.1	30.0	29.8

SOURCE: U.S. Department of Education, Center for Education Statistics, <u>Digest of
Education Statistics, 1995</u>; p. 77, table 66 (data from U.S. Department of
Education's, National Center for Education Statistics, *Schools and
Staffing Survey, 1993-94*). ED 1.113\995

NOTES: 'Total' includes other races and ethnic groups not shown separately. 'White'
excludes persons of Hispanic origin.

UNITS: Percent, as a percent of all public elementary and secondary school teachers,
100.0%.

Table 4.07 Private Elementary and Secondary School Teachers, by Selected Characteristic, 1993-94

	Hispanic	White	Total
Total number of teachers	12,221	347,811	378,365
Percent of teachers, by highest degree earned			
no degree	11.1%	4.8%	5.2%
associate degree	4.9	1.3	1.5
bachelor's degree	57.4	59.4	59.0
master's degree	19.9	30.2	29.8
education specialist	4.4	2.6	2.9
doctor's	2.3	1.6	1.7
Percent of teachers, by years of full-time teaching experience			
less than 3 years	25.5%	20.4%	20.9%
3-9 years	41.8	33.6	33.9
10-20 years	21.6	30.0	29.6
over 20 years	11.1	16.0	15.6

SOURCE: U.S. Department of Education, Center for Education Statistics, <u>Digest of Education Statistics, 1995</u>; p. 77, table 66 (data from U.S. Department of Education's, National Center for Education Statistics, *Schools and Staffing Survey, 1993-95*). ED 1.113\995

NOTES: 'Total' includes other races and ethnic groups not shown separately. 'White' excludes persons of Hispanic origin.

UNITS: Percent, as a percent of all private elementary and secondary school teachers, 100.0%.

Table 4.08 Percent of Students At or Above Selected Reading Proficiency
Levels by Age, 1999

	Hispanic	White	Total
9-year-olds			
level 150	87%	97%	93%
level 200	44	73	64
level 250	6	20	16
13-year-olds			
level 150	100%	100%	100%
level 200	89	96	93
level 250	43	69	61
level 300	6	18	15
17-year-olds			
level 150	100%	100%	100%
level 200	97	98	98
level 250	68	87	82
level 300	24	46	40

SOURCE: U.S. Department of Education, National Center for Education Statistics,
Digest of Education Statistics, 2000; p. 132, table 113. ED 1.113:000

NOTES: 'Total' includes other races and ethnic groups not shown separately.

UNITS: Reading level shown as scale score on scale: 150=able to follow brief
written directions and carry out simple discrete reading tasks; 200=able
to understand, combine ideas, and make inferences based on short
uncomplicated passages about specific or sequentially related
information; 250=able to search for specific information, interrelate
ideas, and make generalizations about literature, science, and social
studies materials; 300=able to find, understand, summarize, and explain
relatively complicated literary and informational material.

Table 4.09 Percent of Students At or Above Selected Science and Math Proficiency Levels by Age, 1999

	Hispanic	White	Total
Science Proficiency			
9-year-olds			
level 150	94.0%	99.0%	97.0%
level 200	56.0	87.0	77.4
level 250	12.0	39.0	31.4
level 300	na	4.0	3.0
13-year-olds			
level 200	78.0%	97.0%	92.7%
level 250	25.0	69.0	57.9
level 300	2.0	14.0	10.9
level 350	0.0	0.0	0.2
17-year-olds			
level 200	97.0%	99.0%	98.0%
level 250	73.0	93.0	85.0
level 300	27.0	57.0	47.4
level 350	5.0	12.0	9.7
Math Proficiency			
9-year-olds			
level 150	98.0%	100.0%	98.9%
level 200	68.0	89.0	82.5
level 250	11.0	37.0	30.9
level 300	0.0	2.0	1.7
13-year-olds			
level 200	97.0%	99.0%	98.7%
level 250	63.0	87.0	78.8
level 300	8.0	29.0	23.2
level 350	0.0	1.0	0.9
17-year-olds			
level 200	100.0%	100.0%	100.0%
level 250	94.0	99.0	96.8
level 300	38.0	70.0	60.7
level 350	3.0	10.0	8.4

SOURCE: U.S. Department of Education, National Center for Education Statistics, <u>Digest of Education Statistics, 2000</u>; p. 146, table 129; p 140, table 123. ED 1.113:000

NOTES: 'Total' includes other races and ethnic groups not shown separately.

UNITS: Math proficiency scale: 150=performs simple addition and subtraction, 200= use basic operations to solve simple problems, 250=uses intermediate level mathematics skills to solve two-step problems, 300=understands measurement and geometry and solves more complex problems, 350= understands and applies more advanced mathematical concepts.

Table 4.10 Student Use of Computers at School, 1984 - 1997

	Hispanic	White	Total
1984, total	18.6%	30.0%	27.3%
1989, total	34.9	45.7	42.7
1993, total	52.3	61.6	59.0
1997			
Total	61.5	71.1	68.8
Prekindergarten and kindergarten	31.0	38.7	36.5
Grades 1-8	68.3	84.0	79.3
Grades 9-12	63.1	71.9	70.5
1st to 4th year of college	63.3	64.3	64.7
5th or later year of college	54.7	53.8	55.5

SOURCE: U.S. Bureau of the Census, Statistical Abstract of the United States, 1999, p. 184, table 289 (data from U.S. National Center for Education Statistics). C 3.134:999

NOTES: 'Total' includes other races and ethnic groups not shown separately. 'White' excludes Hispanic.

UNITS: Percent of students using computers, as of October.

Table 4.11   Labor Force Status of 2000 High School Graduates and
1999-2000 High School Dropouts, October 2000

	Hispanic	White	Total
2000 high school graduates			
total	208	1,366	1,629
employed	191	1,260	1,473
unemployed	16	105	155
not in labor force	93	854	1,127
1999-2000 high school dropouts			
total	62	280	350
employed	39	210	252
unemployed	22	70	99
not in labor force	39	104	165

SOURCE: U.S. Department Labor, Bureau of Labor Statistics "(Table) 1. Labor force
status of 2000 high school graduates and 1999-2000 high school
dropouts 16 to 24 years old by school enrollment, sex, race, and
Hispanic origin, October 2000";
<http://stats.bls.gov/news.release/hsgec.t01.htm>; (accessed: 21 March
2002)

NOTES: 'High school dropouts' refers to persons who dropped out of school between
October 1999 and October 2000.

UNITS: Number of persons in thousands of persons.

Table 4.12   High School Dropout Rates, Grades 10-12, by Sex, 1975 -1998

| | Hispanic | | | White | | | Total | | |
	Male	female	total	male	female	total	male	female	total
1975	10.1%	11.6%	10.9%	NA	NA	NA	5.4%	6.2%	5.8%
1980	16.9	6.9	11.5	NA	NA	NA	6.6	5.4	6.0
1985	9.3	9.8	9.7	NA	NA	NA	5.4	5.0	5.2
1986	11.7	12.4	11.9	NA	NA	NA	4.3	4.2	4.3
1987	5.0	6.2	5.6	NA	NA	NA	4.4	3.8	4.1
1988	12.3	8.4	10.5	NA	NA	NA	5.2	4.5	4.8
1988	7.6	7.7	7.7	NA	NA	NA	4.2	4.5	4.5
1990	8.7	7.2	8.0	NA	NA	NA	4.1	3.9	4.0
1991	10.4	4.8	7.3	NA	NA	NA	3.8	4.3	4.0
1992	5.8	8.6	7.9	NA	NA	NA	3.8	4.8	4.3
1993	4.8	7.7	6.4	NA	NA	NA	4.4	4.1	4.2
1994	8.4	10.1	9.2	NA	NA	NA	4.9	5.1	5.0
1995	10.9	12.5	11.6	NA	NA	NA	5.8	5.0	5.4
1996	9.2	7.6	8.4	NA	NA	NA	4.6	4.8	4.7
1997	10.4	6.7	8.6	4.0	2.8	3.4	4.7	3.8	4.3
1998	8.6	8.2	8.4	3.5	3.8	3.6	4.3	4.6	4.4

SOURCE: U.S. Bureau of the Census, Current Population Reports: School Enrollment-Social and Economic Characteristics of Students: October 1998 (Update), Series P-20, #521, pp. 1-6, table A-4. C3.186/12:999

NOTES: 'Total' includes other races and ethnic groups not shown separately. 'White' excludes 'Hispanic' persons.

UNITS: Percent, as a percent of all persons 16-24 years of age.

Table 4.13   SAT (Scholastic Aptitude Test) Scores, 1987 - 2000

	Hispanic	White	Total
1986-1987			
SAT-Scholastic Aptitude Test			
verbal score	464	524	507
math score	462	514	501
1995-1996			
SAT-Scholastic Aptitude Test			
verbal score	465	526	505
math score	466	523	508
1997-1998			
SAT-Scholastic Aptitude Test			
verbal score	461	526	505
math score	466	528	512
1999-2000			
SAT-Scholastic Aptitude Test			
verbal score	461	528	505
math score	467	530	514

SOURCE: U.S. Department of Education, National Center for Education Statistics, Digest of Education Statistics, 2000; p. 149, table 133. ED 1.113:000

NOTES: 'Total' includes other races and ethnic groups not shown separately.

UNITS: Average scores, (minimum score, 200; maximum score 800).

Chapter 5: Education -
Postsecondary & Educational Attainment

Table 5.01   Enrollment in Institutions of Higher Education, by Type of Institution, 1980 - 1997

	Hispanic	White	Total
1980			
All institutions	1,107	9,883	12,087
4-year institutions	634	6,275	7,565
2-year institutions	472	3,558	4,521
1986			
All institutions	1,081	9,915	12,501
4-year institutions	615	6,340	7,826
2-year institutions	466	3,575	4,675
1988			
All institutions	1,130	10,283	13,043
4-year institutions	656	6,582	8,175
2-year institutions	473	3,702	4,868
1990			
All institutions	1,223	10,675	13,710
4-year institutions	715	6,757	8,529
2-year institutions	509	3,918	5,181
1992			
All institutions	955.0	10,875.4	14,487.4
4-year institutions	410.0	6,744.3	8,765.0
2-year institutions	545.0	4,131.2	5,722.4
1997			
All institutions	1,200.1	10,160.9	14,345.4
4-year institutions	528.0	6,482.7	8,874.7
2-year institutions	672.1	3,678.2	5,470.7

SOURCE: U.S. Department of Education, Center for Education Statistics, Condition of Education, 1993; p. 345, table 44-1.   ED 1.109:993
U.S. Department of Education, Center for Education Statistics, Digest of Education Statistics, 1999; p. 234, table 209.   ED 1.113:999

NOTES: 'Total' includes other races and ethnic groups not shown separately.
'White' excludes persons of Hispanic origin.

UNITS: Enrollment in thousands of students enrolled.

Table 5.02 Enrollment in Institutions of Higher Education, by State, Fall, 1997

	Hispanic	White	Total
UNITED STATES	1,218,493	10,266,122	14,502,334
Alabama	1,696	154,674	218,785
Alaska	836	21,559	27,915
Arizona	44,614	208,648	292,730
Arkansas	1,251	88,641	112,342
California	406,326	955,696	1,958,200
Colorado	24,728	200,332	252,245
Connecticut	8,154	120,373	153,128
Delaware	999	34,824	44,890
District of Columbia	2,906	35,438	72,397
Florida	99,092	420,529	658,259
Georgia	5,051	203,447	306,238
Hawaii	1,429	15,183	61,514
Idaho	1,773	56,560	61,641
Illinois	67,595	500,787	726,199
Indiana	6,838	252,832	295,517
Iowa	3,044	160,715	180,967
Kansas	7,999	148,335	177,544
Kentucky	1,354	158,464	178,924
Louisiana	5,271	142,688	219,196
Maine	376	52,997	56,368
Maryland	6,750	167,418	261,262
Massachusetts	18,983	315,279	412,620
Michigan	12,125	436,283	549,742
Minnesota	3,844	238,810	269,887
Mississippi	759	85,796	130,561
Missouri	5,536	253,158	302,896
Montana	546	38,242	44,141
Nebraska	2,387	99,226	111,542
Nevada	7,167	56,116	76,417
New Hampshire	1,120	58,976	63,811

continued on the next page

Table 5.02   continued

	Hispanic	White	Total
New Jersey	33,498	217,788	325,754
New Mexico	36,516	57,803	108,560
New York	104,157	665,873	1,024,498
North Carolina	5,478	272,743	373,717
North Dakota	291	34,676	38,937
Ohio	8,201	447,217	537,169
Oklahoma	4,610	132,180	177,157
Oregon	6,022	142,148	169,852
Pennsylvania	11,876	486,970	588,185
Rhode Island	3,089	59,982	72,078
South Carolina	1,816	126,555	176,278
South Dakota	165	34,718	39,042
Tennessee	2,780	199,031	249,805
Texas	209,984	582,361	969,283
Utah	4,603	141,988	157,891
Vermont	571	33,875	36,482
Virginia	9,151	265,443	364,904
Washington	13,278	246,843	315,281
West Virginia	933	80,282	87,965
Wisconsin	6,612	262,482	298,248
Wyoming	1,284	27,485	30,280

SOURCE: U.S. Department of Education, Center for Education Statistics, <u>Digest of Education Statistics, 1999</u>; p. 239, table 213. ED 1.113\999

NOTES: 'Total' includes other races and ethnic groups not shown separately. 'White' excludes Hispanic.

UNITS: Enrollment in number of students enrolled.

Table 5.03 Enrollment Rates of 18 - 24 Year Olds in Institutions of Higher Education, 1975 - 1999

	Hispanic	White	Total
Enrollment as a percent of 18-24 year olds			
1975	20.4%	27.4%	26.3%
1980	16.1	27.3	25.7
1986	17.6	29.7	27.9
1987	17.7	31.9	29.7
1988	17.0	33.1	30.2
1990	16.2	35.2	32.1
1991	17.8	36.8	33.3
1992	21.3	37.3	34.4
1993	21.7	36.8	34.0
1994	18.8	38.1	34.6
1995	20.7	37.9	34.3
1996	20.1	39.5	35.5
1997	22.4	40.6	36.2
1998	20.4	40.6	36.5
1999	18.7	39.4	35.6
Enrollment as a percent of high school graduates			
1975	33.0%	32.3%	32.5%
1980	27.6	32.1	31.8
1986	28.3	34.5	34.0
1987	26.6	37.5	36.4
1988	29.1	38.6	37.2
1990	26.8	39.2	37.7
1991	31.4	41.0	39.3
1992	37.5	42.8	42.0
1993	36.1	42.6	41.6
1994	33.1	43.7	42.3
1995	35.2	44.0	42.3
1996	34.5	45.1	43.4
1997	36.1	46.8	44.6
1998	33.9	46.9	45.2
1999	31.6	45.3	43.7

Source: U.S. Department of Education, National Center for Education Statistics, Digest of Education Statistics, 2000 p. 216, table 187. ED 1.113\000

NOTES: 'Total' includes other races and ethnic groups not shown separately. 'White' does not include Hispanic.

UNITS: Percent as a percent of 18-24 year olds, and high school graduates as shown, 100.0%.

Table 5.04 Enrollment of Persons 14 - 34 Years Old in Institutions of
Higher Education, by Sex, 1975 - 1999

	Enrollment			percent distribution		
	Hispanic	White	Total	Hispanic	White	Total
1975						
Total	927	8,141	9,697	9.6%	84.0%	100.0%
men	433	4,566	5,342	4.5	47.1	55.1
women	494	3,576	4,355	5.1	36.9	44.9
1980						
Total	996	8,453	10,181	9.8%	83.0%	100.0%
men	431	4,225	5,193	4.2	41.5	51.0
women	565	4,228	5,244	5.5	41.5	49.0
1985						
Total	1,036	8,781	10,863	9.5%	80.0%	100.0%
men	458	4,361	5,345	4.2	40.1	49.2
women	578	4,420	5,518	5.3	40.7	50.8
1990						
Total	1,167	8,892	11,303	10.3%	78.7%	100.0%
men	508	4,289	na	4.5	38.0	na
women	659	4,594	na	5.8	40.6	na
1993						
Total	1,227	8,592	11,409	10.8%	75.3%	100.0%
men	515	4,168	na	4.5	36.5	na
women	713	4,424	na	6.2	38.8	na
1999						
Total	1,081	8,853	12,506	8.6%	70.8%	100.0%
men	472	4,310	na	3.8	34.5	na
women	609	4,543	na	4.9	36.3	na

SOURCE: U.S. Department of Education, Center for Education Statistics, <u>Digest of Education Statistics, 2000</u>; p. 243, table 213. ED 1.113\000

NOTES: 'Total' includes other races and ethnic groups not shown separately. 'White' excludes Hispanic.

UNITS: Enrollment in thousands of students enrolled; percent as a percentage of 14-34 year olds, by sex as shown, 100.0%.

Table 5.05   School Enrollment by Attendance Status, Type and Control of
School, Fall, 2000

	Hispanic	White	Total
Total enrolled			
two-year college			
full time	285	1,425	2,193
part time	221	1,119	1,688
four-year college			
full time	491	4,810	6,698
part time	231	1,169	1,822
graduate college			
full time	97	870	1,268
part time	101	1,243	1,645
Total public			
two-year college			
full time	256	1,328	2,010
part time	218	1,037	1,581
four-year college			
full time	395	3,504	4,971
part time	203	959	1,482
graduate college			
full time	87	532	839
part time	59	842	1,125
Total private			
two-year college			
full time	29	97	184
part time	3	82	107
four-year college			
full time	96	1,306	1,726
part time	28	210	340
graduate college			
full time	10	339	429
part time	42	401	519

SOURCE: U.S. Bureau of the Census, "Current Population Reports: School Enrollment, (Table) 9.
School Enrollment of the Population 15 Years Old and Over, by Attendance Status, Type
and Control of School, Age, Sex, Race and Hispanic Origin: October 2000;" published 1
June 2001, <http://www.census.gov/population/socdemo/school/ppl-148/tab09.txt>

NOTES: 'Total' includes other races and ethnic groups not shown separately. 'White'
excludes 'Hispanic' persons.

UNITS: Enrollment in thousands of students.

Table 5.06 College Enrollment, October 2000

	Hispanic	White	Total
total enrolled	1,426	10,636	15,314
year enrolled in college			
1st year	453	2,540	3,823
2nd year	348	2,487	3,609
3rd year	228	1,881	2,711
4th year	200	1,615	2,257
5th year	67	708	994
6th year or higher	131	1,406	1,919

SOURCE: U.S. Bureau of the Census, "Current Population Reports: School Enrollment, (Table) 10. Attendance Status of College Students 15 Years Old and Over, by Age, Sex, Year and Type of College, Race and Hispanic Origin: October 2000;" published 1 June 2001, <http://www.census.gov/population/socdemo/school/ppl-148/tab10.txt>

NOTES: 'Total' includes other races and ethnic groups not shown separately. College enrollment at the undergraduate level in two and four year institutions. 'White' excludes 'Hispanic' persons.

UNITS: College enrollment in thousands of students. Institutions of Higher Education, by Sex, 1975 - 1990

Table 5.07 Undergraduates Receiving Financial Aid: Average Amount
Awarded per Student, by Type and Source of Aid, 1995-96

	Hispanic	White	Total
1995-96			
All full-time, full-year enrolled undergraduates	588	4,500	6,306
undergraduates receiving:			
any aid			
total	$ 5,999	$ 6,836	$ 6,832
- from federal source	4,644	5,549	5,362
- from non-federal sources	3,328	3,848	3,883
grants			
total	$ 3,486	$ 3,762	$ 3,864
- from federal source	2,113	1,894	2,001
- from non-federal sources	3,017	3,541	3,599
loans			
total	$ 4,168	$ 4,437	$ 4,345
- from federal source	4,137	4,366	4,288
- from non-federal sources	2,235	2,912	2,747
work-study funds			
total	$ 1,152	$ 1,367	$ 1,371

SOURCE: U.S. Department of Education, Center for Education Statistics, Digest of Education Statistics, 1998; p. 339, table 315. ED 1.113\998

NOTES: 'Total' includes other races and ethnic groups not shown separately. 'White' excludes Hispanic persons.

UNITS: Average 1995-96 award in dollars per student, for students enrolled in Fall, 1995. Number of undergraduates, in thousands.

Table 5.08   Employment Status of Students 16 - 24 Years of Age,
Enrolled in School, 1996

	Hispanic	White	Total
All students 16-24 years of age enrolled in school	1,644	11,708	14,904
in the civilian labor force			
number	653	6,164	7,286
percent	39.7%	52.6%	48.9%
employed	531	5,546	6,448
unemployed	122	618	838
All high school students 16-24 years of age enrolled in school	1,034	5,960	7,687
in the civilian labor force			
number	284	2,628	3,087
percent	27.4%	44.1%	40.2%
employed	206	2,234	2,559
unemployed	78	394	528
All college students 16-24 years of age enrolled in school	609	5,748	7,217
in the civilian labor force			
number	369	3,536	4,199
percent	60.5%	61.5%	58.2%
employed	325	3,312	3,889
unemployed	44	224	310

SOURCE: U.S. Department of Labor, Bureau of Labor Statistics, *Employment and Earnings*, January, 1997; p. 166, table 7, (data from the Current Population Survey). L 2.41/2:37/1:997

NOTES: 'Total' includes other races and ethnic groups not shown separately.

UNITS: Number of students in thousands; percent as a percent of the civilian noninstitutional population 16-24 years of age.

Table 5.09 Enrollment in Schools of Medicine, Dentistry and Related Fields, 1980-81 and 1998-99

	Hispanic	White	Total
1980-81			
allopathic medicine	4.2%	85.0%	100.0%
osteopathic medicine	1.1	94.9	"
podiatry	1.5	91.3	"
dentistry	2.3	88.5	"
optometry	1.8	91.4	"
pharmacy	2.1	88.6	"
veterinary medicine	1.1	95.2	"
registered nursing	na	na	"
1998-99			
dentistry	4.9%	66.4%	100.0%
allopathic medicine	6.7	66.2	"
osteopathic medicine	3.7	77.1	"
registered nursing	3.9	81.0	"
optometry	5.1	68.1	"
pharmacy	3.5	67.3	"
podiatry	4.0	72.0	"

SOURCE: U.S. Department of Health and Human Services, Health United States, 1992, p. 150, table 105; 2001, (Centers for Disease Control and Prevention, National Center for Health Statistics) pp. 318-319 table 106 (data from the Association of American Medical Colleges, American Association of Colleges of Osteopathic Medicine, National League for Nursing, American Association of Colleges of Podiatric Medicine, American Dental Association American Optometric Association, American Association of Colleges of Pharmacy, Association of American Veterinary Medical Colleges). HE 20.6223:(year)

NOTES: 'Total' includes other races and ethnic groups not shown separately. 'White' excludes Hispanic persons.

UNITS: Enrollment as a percentage of all students enrolled, 100.0%.

Table 5.10   Earned Degrees Conferred, by Type of Degree, 1979 - 1998

	Hispanic	White	Total
1979			
Bachelor's degrees	60,130	799,617	916,347
Master's degrees	19,393	249,051	299,887
Doctor's degrees	1,267	26,128	32,664
First Professional degrees	2,836	62,430	68,611
1981			
Bachelor's degrees	60,673	807,319	934,800
Master's degrees	17,133	241,216	294,183
Doctor's degrees	1,265	25,908	32,839
First Professional degrees	2,931	64,551	71,340
1985			
Bachelor's degrees	57,473	826,106	968,311
Master's degrees	13,939	223,628	280,421
Doctor's degrees	1,154	23,934	32,307
First Professional degrees	3,029	63,219	71,057
1991-92			
Bachelor's degrees	40,761	936,771	1,129,833
Master's degrees	9,358	268,371	348,682
Doctor's degrees	811	25,813	40,090
First Professional degrees	2,766	59,800	72,129
1997-98			
Bachelor's degrees	65,937	900,317	1,183,033
Master's degrees	16,215	307,587	429,296
Doctor's degrees	1,270	28,747	45,925
First Professional degrees	3,547	59,273	78,353

SOURCE: U.S. Department of Education, Center for Education Statistics, 1989
Education Indicators, pp. 228-229, table 2:5-1. ED 1.109:989
U.S. Department of Education, Center for Education Statistics, Digest of
Education Statistics, 1994, pp. 276-288, tables 252-264; 2001; p. 313,
table 266; p. 316, table 269; p. 319, table 272; p. 322, table 275. ED
1.113\9(year)

NOTES: 'Total' includes other races and ethnic groups not shown separately.
'White' excludes Hispanic persons. 'First professional Degrees' include
degrees awarded in chiropractic, dentistry, law, medicine, optometry,
osteopathy, pharmacy, podiatry, theology, and veterinary medicine.

UNITS: Earned degrees conferred in number of degrees.

Table 5.11   Associate Degrees Conferred, by Major Field of Study, 1997-98

	Hispanic	White	Total
All Fields, Total	45,627	411,336	555,538
agriculture and natural resources	105	6,271	6,673
architecture and related programs	24	214	265
area, ethnic and cultural studies	12	26	104
biological sciences/life sciences	230	1,346	2,113
business	8,391	74,612	104,659
communications	183	1,780	2,368
communications technologies	136	1,153	1,602
computer and information sciences	1,157	9,317	13,870
construction trades	79	1,817	2,172
education	1,158	6,519	9,278
engineering	189	1,516	2,149
engineering related technologies	2,764	24,072	32,748
English language and literature/letters	189	932	1,609
foreign languages and literatures	119	334	543
health professions and related sciences	4,625	74,311	92,031
home economics	841	5,680	8,292
law and legal studies	589	5,957	7,797
liberal arts/general studies/humanities	16,767	136,238	186,248
library science	2	78	96
mathematics	124	520	844
mechanics and repairers	876	8,000	10,616
multi/interdisciplinary studies	575	7,363	9,401
parks, recreation, and fitness studies	47	705	895
philosophy and religion	5	79	94
physical sciences	160	1,583	2,286
precision production trades	868	8,840	11,085
protective services	2,639	13,838	19,002
psychology	211	1,245	1,765
public administration and services	477	2,350	4,156
military technologies and R.O.T.C.	1	12	22
social sciences and history	591	2,600	4,196
theological studies/religious vocations	20	408	570
transportation	88	788	1,009
visual and performing arts	1,385	10,832	14,980

SOURCE: U.S. Department of Education, National Center for Education Statistics, *Digest of Education Statistics, 2000*; p. 311, table 264. ED 1.113\000

NOTES: 'Total' includes other races and ethnic groups not shown separately. 'White' excludes Hispanic persons.

UNITS: Earned Associate degrees conferred in number of degrees.

Table 5.12 Bachelor's Degrees Conferred, by Major Field of Study, 1997-98

	Hispanic	White	Total
All Fields, Total	65,937	900,317	1,183,033
agriculture and natural resources	651	20,797	23,284
architecture and related programs	534	5,551	7,652
area, ethnic and cultural studies	730	3,626	6,150
biological sciences/life sciences	3,207	47,070	65,868
business	12,487	170,139	233,119
communications	2,440	39,092	49,385
communications technologies	25	535	729
computer and information sciences	1,211	17,414	26,852
construction trades	1	163	182
education	4,369	90,389	105,968
engineering	3,229	41,521	59,910
engineering related technologies	490	10,797	13,727
English language and literature/letters	2,457	40,889	49,708
foreign languages and literatures	2,365	10,260	14,451
health professions and related sciences	3,324	67,502	84,379
home economics	585	14,364	17,296
law and legal studies	123	1,532	2,017
liberal arts/general studies/humanities	2,764	24,347	33,202
library science	1	63	73
mathematics	636	9,247	12,328
mechanics and repairers	7	64	91
multi/interdisciplinary studies	2,538	18,908	26,163
parks, recreation, and fitness studies	788	14,204	16,781
philosophy and religion	430	6,739	8,207
physical sciences	622	15,091	19,416
precision production trades	10	327	407
protective services	2,182	18,087	25,076
psychology	5,192	55,691	73,972
public administration and services	1,499	13,969	20,408
military technologies and R.O.T.C.	0	3	3
social sciences and history	8,167	92,951	125,040
theological studies/religious vocations	167	5,240	5,903
transportation	155	2,642	3,206
visual and performing arts	2,551	41,103	52,077

SOURCE: U.S. Department of Education, National Center for Education Statistics, Digest of Education Statistics, 2000; p. 313, table 266. ED 1.113\000

NOTES: 'Total' includes other races and ethnic groups not shown separately. 'White' excludes Hispanic persons.

UNITS: Earned Bachelor's degrees conferred in number of degrees.

Table 5.13 Master's Degrees Conferred, by Major Field of Study, 1997-98

	Hispanic	White	Total
All Fields, Total	16,215	307,587	429,296
agriculture and natural resources	102	3,303	4,475
architecture and related programs	180	2,823	4,347
area, ethnic and cultural studies	106	1,075	1,617
biological sciences/life sciences	174	4,371	6,261
business	3,247	69,027	102,171
communications	195	3,674	5,611
communications technologies	22	316	564
computer and information sciences	194	4,247	11,246
construction trades	0	5	16
education	5,229	93,116	114,691
engineering	738	12,652	25,936
engineering related technologies	28	839	1,136
English language and literature/letters	257	6,489	7,795
foreign languages and literatures	344	1,808	2,927
health professions and related sciences	1,264	31,218	39,260
home economics	120	2,234	2,914
law and legal studies	96	1,374	3,228
liberal arts/general studies/humanities	85	2,274	2,801
library science	90	4,231	4,871
mathematics	90	2,124	3,643
multi/interdisciplinary studies	94	2,094	2,677
parks, recreation, and fitness studies	55	1,695	2,024
philosophy and religion	39	1,021	1,307
physical sciences	117	3,270	5,361
precision production trades	2	6	15
protective services	67	1,534	2,000
psychology	730	10,894	13,747
public administration and services	1,445	18,036	25,144
military technologies and R.O.T.C.	0	0	0
social sciences and history	590	9,933	14,938
theological studies/religious vocations	115	3,535	4,692
transportation	15	658	736
visual and performing arts	385	7,711	11,145

SOURCE: U.S. Department of Education, National Center for Education Statistics, Digest of Education Statistics, 2000; p. 316, table 269. ED 1.113\000

NOTES: 'Total' includes other races and ethnic groups not shown separately. 'White' excludes Hispanic persons.

UNITS: Earned Master's degrees conferred in number of degrees.

Table 5.14 Doctor's Degrees Conferred, by Major Field of Study, 1997-98

	Hispanic	White	Total
All Fields, Total	1,270	28,747	45,925
agriculture and natural resources	20	590	1,302
architecture and related programs	2	66	131
area, ethnic and cultural studies	3	112	181
biological sciences/life sciences	126	2,970	4,961
business	30	807	1,290
communications	6	259	354
communications technologies	0	3	5
computer and information sciences	9	410	858
education	273	4,943	6,729
engineering	106	2,407	5,980
engineering related technologies	0	5	14
English language and literature/letters	47	1,342	1,639
foreign languages and literatures	87	566	959
health professions and related sciences	66	1,639	2,484
home economics	8	313	424
law and legal studies	2	27	66
liberal arts/general studies/humanities	2	70	87
library science	0	35	48
mathematics	24	579	1,259
multi/interdisciplinary studies	20	341	508
parks, recreation, and fitness studies	1	91	129
philosophy and religion	14	455	585
physical sciences	54	2,548	4,571
precision production trades	0	0	0
protective services	3	19	39
psychology	186	3,345	4,073
public administration and services	21	348	499
military technologies and R.O.T.C.	0	0	0
social sciences and history	102	2,673	4,127
theological studies/religious vocations	35	949	1,460
transportation	0	0	0
visual and performing arts	23	835	1,163

SOURCE: U.S. Department of Education, National Center for Education Statistics, Digest of Education Statistics, 2000; p. 319, table 272. ED 1.113\000

NOTES: 'Total' includes other races and ethnic groups not shown separately. 'White' excludes Hispanic persons.

UNITS: Earned Doctor's degrees conferred in number of degrees.

Table 5.15   First Professional Degrees Conferred, by Field of Study, 1997-98

	Hispanic	White	Total
All Fields, Total	3,547	59,273	78,353
Dentistry	143	2,639	4,032
Medicine	773	10,558	15,424
Optometry	57	871	1,274
Osteopathic medicine	82	1,697	2,110
Pharmacy	75	2,440	3,660
Podiatry	30	434	594
Veterinary medicine	64	2,007	2,193
Chiropractic medicine	114	2,943	3,735
Law	2,085	31,012	39,331
Theological professions	122	4,556	5,873

SOURCE: U.S. Department of Education, National Center for Education Statistics, Digest of Education Statistics, 2000; p. 322, table 275. ED 1.113\000

NOTES: 'Total' includes other races and ethnic groups not shown separately. 'White' excludes Hispanic persons.

UNITS: Earned first professional degrees conferred, in number of degrees.

Table 5.16   Educational Attainment: Years of School Completed by Persons 25 Years Old and Older, 2000

	Hispanic	White	Total
All persons 25 years old and over	17,150	147,067	175,230
percent of the population:			
not a high school graduate	43.0%	15.1%	15.8%
high school graduate	27.9	33.4	33.1
with some college, no degree	13.5	17.4	17.6
with associate's degree	5.0	8.0	7.8
with bachelor's degree	7.3	17.3	17.0
with advanced degree	3.3	8.8	8.6

SOURCE: U.S. Bureau of the Census, Statistical Abstract of the United States, 2001, p. 140, table 217. C 3.134:001

NOTES: 'Total' includes other races and ethnic groups not shown separately. Data as of March.

UNITS: Percent as a percent of the population 25 years old and older; number in thousands of persons 25 years old and older.

Table 5.17   College Completion, Persons 25 Years Old and Older, by Sex, 1970 - 2000

	<u>Hispanic</u>	<u>White</u>	<u>Total</u>
1970			
total	na%	11.6%	11.0%
men	na	15.0	14.1
women	na	8.6	8.2
1975			
total	6.3	14.5	13.9
men	8.3	18.4	17.6
women	4.6	11.0	10.6
1980			
total	7.9	17.8	17.0
men	9.7	22.1	20.9
women	6.2	14.0	13.6
1985			
total	8.5	16.0	19.4
men	9.7	20.0	23.1
women	7.3	24.0	16.0
1990			
total	9.2	22.0	21.3
men	9.8	25.3	24.4
women	8.7	19.0	18.4
2000			
total	10.6	28.1	25.6
men	10.7	30.8	27.8
women	10.6	25.5	23.6

SOURCE: U.S. Bureau of the Census, <u>Current Population Reports: Educational Attainment in the United States: March 1998 (Update)</u>, Series P-20, #513, table 1, pp. 1-5. C3.186/23:998 <http://www.census.gov
U.S. Bureau of the Census, <u>Current Population Reports: Educational Attainment in the United States: March 2000 (Update)</u>, Series P-20, #536, pp. 1-8, 11-14, table 1a. C3.186/23:000 <www.census.gov>

NOTES: 'Total' includes other races not shown separately. 'White' does not include persons of Hispanic origin.

UNITS: Percent as a percent of all persons 25 years old and older completing four or more years of college (1970-1991) or Bachelor's degree or more (1992 and later).

Table 5.18 Educational Attainment of the Hispanic Population, 25 Years Old and Over, by Type of Origin, 2000

	Mexican	Puerto Rican	Cuban	Central/ South American	Other Hispanic	Total Hispanic
less than 9th grade	32.3%	17.5%	18.1%	22.3%	15.1%	27.3%
9th to 12th grade (no diploma)	16.8	18.1	8.9	13.4	13.3	15.7
high school graduate	26.4	29.5	33.0	29.5	32.3	27.9
some college or associate degree	17.7	21.9	17.0	17.5	24.8	18.5
bachelor's degree	5.1	8.6	13.9	11.8	8.9	7.3
advanced degree	1.8	4.4	9.2	5.6	5.6	3.3

SOURCE: U.S. Bureau of the Census, "Current Population Reports: The Hispanic Population of the United States, 2000, (Table) 7.1. Educational Attainment of the Population 25 Years and Over by Sex, Hispanic Origin and Race: March 2000," published March 6, 2001.
<http: //www..census.gov/population/socdemo/Hispanic/p20-535/tab07-1.txt>

NOTES: Total population includes other races and ethnic groups not shown separately. 'Other Hispanic origin' includes persons from Spain and persons identifying themselves generally as Hispanic, Spanish, Spanish-American, Hispano, Latino, etc.

UNITS: Persons completing educational levels in percent as a percent of all persons, by origin, 100.0%.

Table 5.19   Highest Educational Level and Degree Earned, Persons 18
Years Old and Older, 1999

	Hispanic	White	Total
Total civilian noninstitutional population	20,363	147,400	199,721
less than 7 years of elementary school	3,744	1,805	6,709
7 or 8 years of elementary school	1,237	4,175	6,346
1 to 3 years of high school	3,184	11,593	18,793
4 years of high school	675	1,575	2,964
high school graduate	5,593	50,077	66,054
some college	3,163	29,263	39,087
Associate degree	872	11,324	14,114
Bachelor's degree	1,387	25,590	31,256
Master's degree	319	8,167	9,836
First professional degree	111	2,112	2,514
Doctorate degree	79	1,718	2,049

SOURCE: U.S. Department of Education, National Center for Education Statistics,
Digest of Education Statistics, 2000; p. 18, table 9 (data from U.S.
Bureau of the Census, *Current Population Reports*, unpublished data.)
ED 1.113\000

NOTES: 'Total' includes other races and ethnic groups not shown separately.
'White' excludes persons of Hispanic origin.

UNITS: Persons in thousands, by highest educational level attained.

Table 5.20 Employment of 12th Graders, 1992

	Hispanic	White	Total
Most recent type of work for **employed students**, total	100.0%	100.0%	100.0%
lawn work or odd jobs	0.9	2.5	2.2
food service	24.8	22.8	24.0
delivery person	1.1	1.5	1.6
baby-sitter or child care	2.2	4.8	4.3
camp counselor/life guard	0.5	0.9	0.7
farm worker	1.1	2.7	2.2
mechanic	1.5	1.5	1.4
grocery clerk or cashier	11.6	14.8	14.5
beautician	0.3	0.1	0.2
house cleaning	2.0	0.8	0.9
construction	1.9	2.1	2.0
office or clerical	8.7	6.3	6.9
health services	1.1	1.6	1.6
salesperson	11.9	12.0	11.8
warehouse worker	1.7	2.2	2.1
other	28.8	23.5	23.5

SOURCE: U.S. Department of Education, Center for Education Statistics, Digest of
            Education Statistics, 1994; p. 403, table 373. Data from U.S. Department
            of Education, National Center for Education Statistics, "National
            Education Longitudinal Study of 1988," Second Follow-up. ED 1.113\994

NOTES: 'Total' includes other races/ethnic groups not shown separately.

UNITS: Percent as a percent of all high school seniors of a given race/ethnicity who
            were employed in 1992.

Chapter 6: Government & Elections

Table 6.01 Hispanic Elected Public Officials, by Type of Office Held, 1985 - 2000

	State executives & legislators	County & municipal officials	Judicial & law enforcement	Education & school boards	Total
1985	119	1,316	517	1,185	3,147
1986	122	1,352	530	1,188	3,202
1987	127	1,412	568	1,199	3,317
1988	124	1,425	574	1,226	3,360
1989	133	1,724	575	1,341	3,783
1990	134	1,819	583	1,458	4,004
1991	140	1,867	596	1,588	4,202
1992	139	1,908	628	2,308	4,994
1993	182	2,023	633	2,332	5,170
1994	199	2,197	651	2,412	5,459
2000	223	1,846	454	2,682	5,205

SOURCE: U.S. Bureau of the Census, Statistical Abstract of the United States, 2001, p. 250, table 400 (data from National Association of Latino Elected and Appointed Officials, *National Roster of Hispanic Elected Officials*). C 3.134:001

NOTES: Data as of September. Total includes US Representatives not shown separately.

UNITS: Number of Hispanic elected public officials.

Table 6.02   Voting Age Population, Registration, and Voting, 1972 - 2000

	Hispanic	White	Total
Voting age population			
1972	5.6	121.2	136.2
1974	6.1	125.1	141.3
1976	6.6	129.3	146.5
1978	6.8	133.4	151.6
1980	8.8	137.7	157.1
1982	8.8	143.6	165.5
1984	9.5	146.8	170.0
1986	11.8	149.9	173.9
1988	12.9	152.8	178.1
1990	13.8	155.6	182.1
1992	14.7	157.8	185.7
1994	17.5	160.3	190.3
1996	18.4	162.8	193.7
1998	20.3	165.8	198.2
2000	21.6	168.8	202.6
Presidential election years			
percent reporting registration			
1972	44.4%	73.4%	72.3%
1976	37.8	68.3	66.7
1980	36.3	68.4	66.9
1984	40.1	69.6	68.3
1988	35.5	67.9	66.6
1992	35.0	70.1	68.2
1996	35.7	67.7	65.9
2000	57.3	70.4	69.5
percent reporting voting			
1972	37.4%	64.5	63.0%
1976	31.8	60.9	59.2
1980	29.9	60.9	59.2
1984	32.6	61.4	59.9
1988	28.8	59.1	57.4
1992	28.9	63.6	61.3
1996	26.7	56.0	54.2
2000	45.1	60.5	59.5

continued on the next page

Table 6.02   continued

	Hispanic	White	Total
Congressional election years			
percent reporting registration			
1974	34.9%	63.5%	62.6%
1978	32.9	63.8	62.6
1982	35.3	65.6	64.1
1986	35.9	65.3	64.3
1990	32.3	63.8	62.2
1994	31.3	64.6	62.5
1998	33.7	63.9	62.1
percent reporting voting			
1974	22.9%	46.3%	44.7%
1978	23.5	47.3	45.9
1982	25.3	49.9	48.5
1986	24.2	47.0	46.0
1990	21.0	46.7	45.0
1994	20.2	47.3	45.0
1998	20.0	43.3	41.9

SOURCE: U.S. Bureau of the Census, Statistical Abstract of the United States, 1989; p. 257, table 432 , 1999; p. 300, table 487 (data from U.S. Bureau of the Census, *Current Population Reports*, Series P-20). C 3.134:9(year)

U.S. Bureau of the Census, Current Population Reports: Voting and Registration in the Election of November, 1988, Series P-20, #440, pp. 48-49, table 8. C 3.186/3-2:989

U.S. Bureau of the Census, Current Population Reports: Voting and Registration in the Election of November, 1990, Series P-20, #453, pp. 16-17, table 2. C 3.186/3-2:990

U.S. Bureau of the Census, Current Population Reports: Voting and Registration in the Election of November, 1992, Series P-20, #466, pp. 4-5, table 2. C 3.186/3-2:992

Voting and Registration Data from the November 1994 Current Population Survey, Table 1, Table VI. <www.census.gov>

U.S. Bureau of the Census, Current Population Reports: Voting and Registration in the Election of November, 1996, Series P-20, #504, table 23. C 3.186/3-2:996

U.S. Bureau of the Census, Current Population Reports: Voting and Registration in the Election of November 2000, Series P-20, #542, P. 5, Table A. C 3.186/3-2:000

NOTES: 'Total' includes other races and ethnic groups not shown separately.

UNITS: Voting age population in millions of persons; percent reporting registration and percent reporting voting as a percent of the voting age population.

Table 6.03   Voting Age Population, Selected Characteristics, 1990

	Hispanic	White	Total
Voting age population, 1990			
by age			
total 18 years and over	13,756	155,587	182,118
18-20 years old	1,139	8,722	10,800
21-24 years old	1,572	11,635	14,031
25-34 years old	4,180	35,682	45,652
35-44 years old	2,886	32,281	37,889
45-54 years old	1,707	21,983	25,648
55-64 years old	1,200	18,477	21,223
65-74 years old	728	16,180	18,126
75 years and over	344	10,627	11,748
by sex			
male	6,787	74,625	86,621
female	6,968	80,962	95,496
by years of school completed			
elementary			
0-4 years of school	1,417	2,617	3,669
5-7 years of school	1,903	5,096	6,445
8 years of school	910	6,564	7,617
high school			
1-3 years high school	2,353	16,733	20,956
4 years high school	4,160	61,342	71,492
college			
1-3 years college	1,881	31,481	36,300
4 years college	679	18,900	21,350
5 or more years college	452	12,855	14,288
by family income			
under $5,000	801	4,503	6,799
$5,000-$9,999	1,425	6,978	9,808
$10,000-$14,999	1,877	11,049	13,759
$15,000-$19,999	1,185	8,677	10,496
$20,000-$24,999	1,162	10,619	12,304
$25,000-$34,999	1,832	20,827	23,627
$35,000-$49,999	1,384	22,698	25,367
$50,000 and over	1,231	30,330	32,818
income not reported	768	9,555	11,576

SOURCE: U.S. Bureau of the Census, Current Population Reports: Voting and Registration in the Election of November, 1990, Series P-20, #453, pp. 16-17, table 2; pp. 47-48, table 8; p. 64, table 13.
C 3.186/3-2:990

NOTES: 'Total' includes other races and ethnic groups not shown separately.

UNITS: Voting age population in thousands of persons.

Table 6.04 Selected Characteristics of Persons Registered to Vote, 1990

	Hispanic	White	Total
Persons registered to vote, 1990			
by age			
total 18 years and over	32.3%	63.8%	62.2%
18-20 years old	17.2	37.0	35.4
21-24 years old	20.9	43.1	43.3
25-34 years old	27.4	53.2	52.0
35-44 years old	34.8	67.2	65.5
45-54 years old	38.3	71.3	69.8
55-64 years old	45.5	74.9	73.5
65-74 years old	56.6	79.7	78.3
75 years and over	46.0	74.8	73.7
by sex			
male	30.0%	63.0%	61.2%
female	34.5	64.6	63.1
by years of school completed			
0-4 years of elementary school	15.3%	26.4%	29.5%
5-7 years of elementary school	15.8	38.7	41.1
8 years of elementary school	28.1	54.3	53.3
1-3 years of high school	24.6	48.2	47.9
4 years of high school	36.6	61.2	60.0
1-3 years of college	50.6	70.2	68.7
4 years of college	51.1	77.1	74.5
5 or more years of college	59.3	83.5	81.5
by households income			
under $5,000	28.2%	53.1%	50.7%
$5,000-$9,999	22.7	47.6	48.3
$10,000-$14,999	23.9	55.4	54.8
$15,000-$19,999	29.0	57.5	56.8
$20,000-$24,999	21.7	59.0	58.0
$25,000-$34,999	37.7	65.0	63.9
$35,000-$49,999	46.5	69.4	68.3
$50,000 and over	51.7	77.8	76.4
income not reported	29.6	59.7	57.6

SOURCE: U.S. Bureau of the Census, Current Population Reports: Voting and Registration in the Election of November, 1990, Series P-20, #453, pp. 16-17, table 2; pp. 47-48, table 8; p. 64, table 13. C 3.186/3-2:990

NOTES: 'Total' includes other races and ethnic groups not shown separately.

UNITS: Person reporting registration to vote as a percent of the voting age population, 100.0%.

Table 6.05   Selected Characteristics of Persons Voting, 1990

	Hispanic	White	Total
Persons voting, 1990			
by age			
total 18 years and over	21.0%	46.7%	45.0%
18-20 years old	10.1	19.4	18.4
21-24 years old	7.8	21.8	22.0
25-34 years old	16.5	34.9	33.8
35-44 years old	24.2	50.0	48.4
45-54 years old	25.4	54.9	53.2
55-64 years old	33.5	60.4	58.9
65-74 years old	43.8	65.7	64.1
75 years and over	33.4	55.8	54.5
by sex			
male	19.4%	46.4%	44.6%
female	22.6	46.9	45.4
by years of school completed			
elementary			
0-4 years of school	9.4%	14.8%	16.5%
5-7 years of school	11.3	23.7	25.7
8 years of school	15.6	35.7	34.8
high school			
1-3 years high school	13.5	31.3	30.9
4 years high school	22.5	43.6	42.2
college			
1-3 years college	36.0	51.4	50.0
4 years college	38.8	61.6	59.0
5 or more years college	45.8	69.6	67.8
by households income			
under $5,000	14.9%	35.1%	32.2%
$5,000-$9,999	14.6	31.3	30.9
$10,000-$14,999	14.5	38.5	37.7
$15,000-$19,999	16.6	39.9	38.8
$20,000-$24,999	14.9	42.5	41.3
$25,000-$34,999	26.3	47.5	46.4
$35,000-$49,999	29.8	51.8	51.0
$50,000 and over	37.8	60.5	59.2
income not reported	19.3	45.1	43.3

SOURCE: U.S. Bureau of the Census, <u>Current Population Reports: Voting and Registration in the Election of November, 1990</u>, Series P-20, #453, pp. 16-17, table 2; pp. 47-48, table 8; p. 64, table 13.
C 3.186/3-2:990

NOTES: 'Total' includes other races and ethnic groups not shown separately.

UNITS: Persons reporting voting as a percent of the voting age population, 100.0%.

Table 6.06   Voting Age Population, Selected Characteristics, 2000

	Hispanic	White	Total
Voting age population, 2000			
Total, 18 years and over	21,598	168,733	202,609
by sex			
male	10,653	69,290	97,087
female	10,945	74,361	105,523
by age			
18-24 years old	4,169	21,295	26,712
25-44 years old	10,640	66,378	81,780
45-64 years old	4,962	52,038	61,352
65-74 years old	1,110	15,493	17,819
75 years and over	718	13,529	14,945
by educational attainment			
less than 9th grade	5,272	10,626	12,894
9th to 12th grade, no diploma	3,931	15,822	20,108
high school graduate or GED	6,295	55,530	66,339
some college or associate degree	4,036	45,923	55,308
bachelor's degree	1,438	27,382	32,254
advanced degree	627	13,450	15,706
by employment status			
in civilian labor force	15,280	115,103	138,378
unemployed	826	3,544	4,944

continued on the next page

Table 6.06   continued

	Hispanic	White	Total
by family income			
less than $5,000	532	1,405	2,230
$5,000-$9,999	998	2,732	4,242
$10,000-$14,999	1,073	5,390	7,286
$15,000-$24,999	3,249	11,568	14,600
$25,000-$34,999	2,934	14,578	17,692
$35,000-$49,999	2,518	18,907	22,349
$50,000-$74.999	2,182	24,250	28,144
$75,000 and over	1,695	31,021	35,030
income not reported	1,304	17,518	20,721

SOURCE: U.S. Bureau of the Census, "Current Population Reports: Voting and Registration in the Election of November, 2000, (Table 2). Reported Voting and Registration, by Race, Hispanic Origin, Sex, and Age, for the United States: November 2000;" published 27 February 2002; <http://www.census.gov/population/socdemo/voting/p20-542/tab02.txt>
U.S. Bureau of the Census, "Current Population Reports: Voting and Registration in the Election of November, 2000, (Table 6). Reported Voting and Registration, by Race, Hispanic Origin, Sex, and Educational Attainment: November 2000;" published 27 February 2002; <http://www.census.gov/population/socdemo/voting/p20-542/tab06.txt>
U.S. Bureau of the Census, "Current Population Reports: Voting and Registration in the Election of November, 2000, (Table 7). Reported Voting and Registration, by Race, Hispanic Origin, Sex, Employment Status and Class of Worker: November 2000;" published 27 February 2002; <http://www.census.gov/population/socdemo/voting/p20-542/tab07.txt>
U.S. Bureau of the Census, "Current Population Reports: Voting and Registration in the Election of November, 2000, (Table 9). Reported Voting and Registration of Family Members, by Race, Hispanic Origin, and Family Income: November 2000;" published 27 February 2002; <http://www.census.gov/population/socdemo/voting/p20-542/tab09.txt>

NOTES: 'Total' includes other races and ethnic groups not shown separately.

UNITS: Voting age population in thousands of persons.

Table 6.07   Selected Characteristics of Persons Registered to Vote, 2000

	Hispanic	White	Total
Voting age population, 2000			
Total, 18 years and over	34.9%	65.6%	63.9%
by sex			
male	31.7	64.0	62.2
female	38.1	67.2	65.6
by age			
18-24 years old	23.2	46.3	45.4
25-44 years old	31.1	61.2	59.6
45-64 years old	45.1	72.7	71.2
65-74 years old	57.2	77.3	76.2
75 years and over	55.9	77.2	76.1
by educational attainment			
less than 9th grade	17.4	34.8	36.1
9th to 12th grade, no diploma	25.4	44.8	45.9
high school graduate or GED	38.0	61.3	60.1
some college or associate degree	51.1	71.8	70.0
bachelor's degree	53.5	79.6	76.3
advanced degree	64.7	83.1	79.4
by employment status			
in civilian labor force	34.2	65.5	64.0
unemployed	22.6	44.9	46.1

continued on the next page

Table 6.07   continued

	Hispanic	White	Total
by family income			
less than $5,000	25.6%	40.7%	44.0
$5,000-$9,999	28.2	45.3	48.8
$10,000-$14,999	26.4	47.5	49.8
$15,000-$24,999	26.3	55.1	54.9
$25,000-$34,999	30.0	61.9	61.0
$35,000-$49,999	41.1	68.8	67.1
$50,000-$74.999	49.3	75.9	73.8
$75,000 and over	63.5	80.7	78.4
income not reported	32.1	55.5	54.2

SOURCE: U.S. Bureau of the Census, "Current Population Reports: Voting and Registration in the Election of November, 2000, (Table 2). Reported Voting and Registration, by Race, Hispanic Origin, Sex, and Age, for the United States: November 2000;" published 27 February 2002; <http://www.census.gov/population/socdemo/voting/p20-542/tab02.txt>
U.S. Bureau of the Census, "Current Population Reports: Voting and Registration in the Election of November, 2000, (Table 6). Reported Voting and Registration, by Race, Hispanic Origin, Sex, and Educational Attainment: November 2000;" published 27 February 2002; <http://www.census.gov/population/socdemo/voting/p20-542/tab06.txt>
U.S. Bureau of the Census, "Current Population Reports: Voting and Registration in the Election of November, 2000, (Table 7). Reported Voting and Registration, by Race, Hispanic Origin, Sex, Employment Status and Class of Worker: November 2000;" published 27 February 2002; <http://www.census.gov/population/socdemo/voting/p20-542/tab07.txt>
U.S. Bureau of the Census, "Current Population Reports: Voting and Registration in the Election of November, 2000, (Table 9). Reported Voting and Registration of Family Members, by Race, Hispanic Origin, and Family Income: November 2000;" published 27 February 2002; <http://www.census.gov/population/socdemo/voting/p20-542/tab09.txt>

NOTES: 'Total' includes other races and ethnic groups not shown separately.

UNITS: Persons registered to vote as a percent of the voting age population, 100.0%..

Table 6.08   Selected Characteristics of Persons Voting, 2000

	<u>Hispanic</u>	<u>White</u>	<u>Total</u>
Voting age population, 2000			
Total, 18 years and over	27.5%	47.4%	41.9%
by sex			
male	25.1	47.3	41.4
female	29.8	47.4	42.4
by age			
18-24 years old	15.4	33.0	32.3
25-44 years old	23.2	51.2	49.8
45-64 years old	38.3	65.6	64.1
65-74 years old	50.9	71.1	69.9
75 years and over	48.7	66.2	64.9
by educational attainment			
less than 9th grade	14.0	25.8	26.8
9th to 12th grade, no diploma	17.4	32.7	33.6
high school graduate or GED	28.7	50.4	49.4
some college or associate degree	41.1	62.0	60.3
bachelor's degree	47.0	73.4	70.3
advanced degree	59.8	79.3	75.5
by employment status			
in civilian labor force	26.7	56.2	54.8
unemployed	15.5	34.6	35.1

continued on the next page

Table 6.08   continued

	Hispanic	White	Total
by family income			
less than $5,000	16.2%	27.3%	28.2%
$5,000-$9,999	20.8	32.5	34.7
$10,000-$14,999	19.7	35.6	37.7
$15,000-$24,999	19.4	43.3	43.4
$25,000-$34,999	23.6	51.8	51.0
$35,000-$49,999	31.5	58.8	57.5
$50,000-$74.999	39.5	67.1	65.2
$75,000 and over	57.0	73.8	71.5
income not reported	27.1	49.6	48.2

SOURCE: U.S. Bureau of the Census, "Current Population Reports: Voting and Registration in the Election of November, 2000, (Table 2). Reported Voting and Registration, by Race, Hispanic Origin, Sex, and Age, for the United States: November 2000;" published 27 February 2002; <http://www.census.gov/population/socdemo/voting/p20-542/tab02.txt>
U.S. Bureau of the Census, "Current Population Reports: Voting and Registration in the Election of November, 2000, (Table 6). Reported Voting and Registration, by Race, Hispanic Origin, Sex, and Educational Attainment: November 2000;" published 27 February 2002; <http://www.census.gov/population/socdemo/voting/p20-542/tab06.txt>
U.S. Bureau of the Census, "Current Population Reports: Voting and Registration in the Election of November, 2000, (Table 7). Reported Voting and Registration, by Race, Hispanic Origin, Sex, Employment Status and Class of Worker: November 2000;" published 27 February 2002; <http://www.census.gov/population/socdemo/voting/p20-542/tab07.txt>
U.S. Bureau of the Census, "Current Population Reports: Voting and Registration in the Election of November, 2000, (Table 9). Reported Voting and Registration of Family Members, by Race, Hispanic Origin, and Family Income: November 2000;" published 27 February 2002; <http://www.census.gov/population/socdemo/voting/p20-542/tab09.txt>

NOTES: 'Total' includes other races and ethnic groups not shown separately.

UNITS: Persons reporting voting as a percent of the voting age population, 100.0%.

Table 6.09 Members of Congress, 1981 - 1995

	Hispanic	White	Total
House of Representatives			
97th Congress, 1981	6	415	435
98th Congress, 1983	8	411	"
99th Congress, 1985	10	412	"
100th Congress, 1987	11	408	"
101st Congress, 1989	10	406	"
102nd Congress, 1991	11	407	"
103rd Congress, 1993	17	393	"
104th Congress, 1995	17	391	"
Senate			
97th Congress, 1981	0	97	100
98th Congress, 1983	0	98	"
99th Congress, 1985	0	98	"
100th Congress, 1987	0	98	"
101st Congress, 1989	0	98	"
102nd Congress, 1991	0	98	"
103rd Congress, 1993	0	97	"
104th Congress, 1995	0	97	"

SOURCE: U.S. Bureau of the Census, Statistical Abstract of the United States, 1995; p. 281, table 444 (data from Congressional Quarterly, Inc.). C 3.134:995

NOTES: 'Total' includes other races and ethnic groups not shown separately.

UNITS: Number of members of the House and Senate respectively, as shown.

Chapter 7: The Labor Force, Employment & Unemployment

Table 7.01   Labor Force Participation of the Civilian Noninstitutional
Population 16 Years Old & Over, by Age, 1985, 1990, 2000

	Hispanic	White	Total
1985			
civilian noninstitutional population			
all persons 16 years old and over	11,915	153,679	178,206
- persons 16-19 years old	1,298	11,900	14,506
- persons 20 years old and over	10,617	141,780	163,700
- persons 65 years old and over	843	24,352	26,977
civilian labor force			
all persons 16 years old and over	7,698	99,926	115,461
- persons 16-19 years old	579	6,841	7,901
- persons 20 years old and over	7,119	93,085	107,560
- persons 65 years old and over	82	2,605	2,907
labor force participation rate			
all persons 16 years old and over	64.6%	65.0%	64.8%
- persons 16-19 years old	44.6	57.5	54.5
- persons 20 years old and over	67.1	65.7	65.7
- persons 65 years old and over	9.7	10.7	10.8

continued on the next page

Table 7.01   continued

	Hispanic	White	Total
1990			
civilian noninstitutional population			
all persons 16 years old and over	14,297	160,415	188,049
- persons 16-19 years old	1,424	11,095	13,794
- persons 20 years old and over	12,873	149,320	174,255
- persons 65 years old and over	na	26,643	29,730
civilian labor force			
all persons 16 years old and over	9576	107,177	124,787
- persons 16-19 years old	672	6,374	7,410
- persons 20 years old and over	8,904	100,803	117,377
- persons 65 years old and over	na	3,189	3,535
labor force participation rate			
all persons 16 years old and over	67.0%	66.8%	66.4%
- persons 16-19 years old	47.2	57.5	53.7
- persons 20 years old and over	69.2	62.8	62.4
- persons 65 years old and over	na	12.0	11.9

continued on the next page

Table 7.01   continued

	Hispanic	White	Total
2000			
civilian noninstitutional population			
all persons 16 years old and over	22,393	174,428	209,699
- persons 16-19 years old	2,341	12,707	16,042
- persons 65 years old and over	1,791	28,947	32,705
civilian labor force			
all persons 16 years old and over	15,368	117,574	140,863
- persons 16-19 years old	1,083	7,075	8,369
- persons 65 years old and over	218	3,749	4,200
labor force participation rate			
all persons 16 years old and over	68.6%	67.4%	67.2%
- persons 16-19 years old	46.3	55.7	52.2
- persons 65 years old and over	12.2	13.0	12.8

SOURCE: U.S. Department of Labor, Bureau of Labor Statistics, Handbook of Labor Statistics, 1989, pp. 13-30, tables 3-5. L 2.3/5:989
U.S. Department of Labor, Bureau of Labor Statistics, *Employment and Earnings,* January, 1991; p. 208, table 39; January, 2001; p. 168-169, table 3; p. 171, table 4 (data from the Current Population Survey). L2.41/2:(vol)/1:(year)

NOTES: 'Total' includes other races and ethnic groups not shown separately.

UNITS: Civilian noninstitutional population and civilian labor force in thousands of persons; participation rate as a percent (the civilian noninstitutional population divided by the civilian labor force).

Table 7.02 Labor Force Participation of the Civilian Noninstitutional Population 16 Years Old and Over, by Sex and Age, 1985, 1990, 2000

	Hispanic		White		Total	
	male	female	male	female	male	female
1985						
civilian noninstitutional population						
all persons 16 years old and over	5,885	6,029	73,373	80,306	84,469	93,736
- persons 16-19 years old	654	644	5,987	5,912	7,275	7,231
- persons 20 years old and over	5,232	5,385	67,386	74,394	77,195	86,506
- persons 65 years old and over	354	489	10,010	14,342	11,084	15,913
civilian labor force						
all persons 16 years old and over	4,729	2,970	56,472	43,455	64,411	51,050
- persons 16-19 years old	334	245	3,576	3,265	4,134	3,767
- persons 20 years old and over	4,395	2,725	52,895	40,190	60,277	47,283
- persons 65 years old and over	53	29	1,595	1,010	1,750	1,156
labor force participation rate						
all persons 16 years old and over	80.3%	49.3%	77.0%	54.1%	76.3%	54.5%
- persons 16-19 years old	51.0	38.1	59.7	55.2	56.8	52.1
- persons 20 years old and over	84.0	50.6	78.5	54.0	78.1	54.7
- persons 65 years old and over	14.9	5.9	15.9	7.0	15.8	7.3

continued on the next page

Table 7.02   continued

	Hispanic		White		Total	
	male	female	male	female	male	female
1990						
civilian noninstitutional population						
all persons 16 years old and over	7,087	7,210	77,082	83,332	89,650	98,399
- persons 16-19 years old	721	703	5,600	5,495	6,947	6,847
- persons 20 years old and over	6,366	6,507	71,482	77,837	82,703	91,552
- persons 65 years old and over	na	na	11,129	15,514	12,392	17,337
civilian labor force						
all persons 16 years old and over	5,755	3,821	58,298	47,879	68,234	56,554
- persons 16-19 years old	401	271	3,329	3,046	3,866	3,544
- persons 20 years old and over	5,354	3,550	54,969	44,833	64,368	53,010
- persons 65 years old and over	na	na	1,865	1,325	2,033	1,502
labor force participation rate						
all persons 16 years old and over	81.2%	53.0%	76.9%	57.5%	76.1%	57.5%
- persons 16-19 years old	55.6	38.5	59.4	55.4	55.7	51.8
- persons 20 years old and over	84.1	54.6	78.3	57.6	77.8	57.9
- persons 65 years old and over	na	na	16.8	8.5	16.4	8.7

continued on the next page

Table 7.02 continued

	Hispanic		White		Total	
	male	female	male	female	male	female
2000						
civilian noninstitutional population all persons 16 years old and over	11,064	11,329	84,647	89,781	100,731	108,968
- persons 16-19 years old	1,205	1,136	6,496	6,211	8,151	7,890
- persons 65 years old and over	759	1,032	12,390	16,557	13,925	18,780
civilian labor force all persons 16 years old and over	8,919	6,449	63,861	53,714	75,247	65,616
- persons 16-19 years old	613	470	3,679	3,396	4,317	4,051
- persons 65 years old and over	138	80	2,198	1,550	2,439	1,762
labor force participation rate all persons 16 years old and over	80.6%	56.9%	75.4%	59.8%	74.7%	60.2%
- persons 16-19 years old	50.9	41.4	56.6	54.7	53.0	51.3
- persons 65 years old and over	18.2	7.7	17.7	9.4	17.5	9.4

SOURCE: U.S. Department of Labor, Bureau of Labor Statistics, <u>Handbook of Labor Statistics, 1989</u>, pp. 13-30, tables 3-5. L 2.3/5:989

U.S. Department of Labor, Bureau of Labor Statistics, *Employment and Earnings*, <u>January, 1991</u>; p. 208, table 39; <u>January, 2001</u>; p. 168-169, table 3; p. 171, table 4 (data from the Current Population Survey). L 2.41/2:(vol)/1:(year)

NOTES: 'Total' includes other races and ethnic groups not shown separately.

UNITS: Civilian noninstitutional population and civilian labor force in thousands of persons; participation rate as a percent (the civilian noninstitutional population divided by the civilian labor force).

Table 7.03 Labor Force Participation of the Hispanic Civilian
Noninstitutional Population 16 Years Old and Over, by Type
of Hispanic Origin, 1985, 1990, 2000

	Mexican	Puerto Rican	Cuban	Central/ South American	Other Hispanic	Total Hispanic
1985						
Total population 16 years and over						
number	6,625	1,721	851	1,248	1,021	11,446
percent	100.0%	100.0%	100.0%	100.0%	100.0%	100.0%
In the labor force						
number	4,427	882	557	853	643	7,362
percent	66.8%	51.2%	65.5%	68.3%	63.0%	64.2%
Male population 16 years and over						
number	3,402	754	413	587	486	5,643
percent	100.0%	100.0%	100.0%	100.0%	100.0%	100.0
In the labor force						
number	2,773	504	308	483	358	4,427
percent	81.5%	66.9%	74.6%	82.3%	73.7%	78.5%
Female population 16 years and over						
number	3,223	967	438	661	534	5,823
percent	100.0%	100.0%	100.0%	100.0%	100.0%	100.0
In the labor force						
number	1,654	378	249	370	584	2,935
percent	51.3%	39.0%	56.9%	55.9%	53.2%	50.4%

continued on the next page

Table 7.03   continued

	Mexican	Puerto Rican	Cuban	Central/ South American	Other Hispanic	Total Hispanic
1990						
Total population 16 years and over						
number	8,696	1,492	839	2,106	1,079	114,212
percent	100.0%	100.0%	100.0%	100.0%	100.0%	100.0%
In the labor force						
number	5,871	805	554	1,509	709	9,449
percent	67.5%	54.0%	66.0%	71.7%	65.7%	66.5%
Male population 16 years and over						
number	4,493	673	402	991	511	7,069
percent	100.0%	100.0%	100.0%	100.0%	100.0%	100.0%
In the labor force						
number	3,647	466	301	829	385	5,629
percent	81.2%	69.2%	74.9%	83.7%	75.3%	79.6%
Female population 16 years and over						
number	4,203	819	438	1,114	568	7,143
percent	100.0%	100.0%	100.0%	100.0%	100.0%	100.0%
In the labor force						
number	2,224	339	253	680	324	3,821
percent	52.9%	41.4%	57.8%	61.0%	57.0%	53.5%

continued on the next page

Table 7.03   continued

	Mexican	Puerto Rican	Cuban	Central/ South American	Other Hispanic	Total Hispanic
2000						
Total population 16 years and over						
number	14,144	2,040	1,073	3,472	1,440	22,170
percent	100.0%	100.0%	100.0%	100.0%	100.0%	100.0%
In the labor force						
number	9,720	1,309	658	2,492	984	15,163
percent	68.7%	64.2%	61.3%	71.8%	68.4%	68.4%
Male population 16 years and over						
number	7,197	959	518	1,618	669	10,961
percent	100.0%	100.0%	100.0%	100.0%	100.0%	100.0%
In the labor force						
number	5,903	667	383	1,361	502	8,817
percent	82.0%	69.6%	74.0%	84.1%	75.1%	80.4%
Female population 16 years and over						
number	6,947	1,081	555	1,854	771	11,209
percent	100.0%	100.0%	100.0%	100.0%	100.0%	100.0%
In the labor force						
number	3,816	642	275	1,131	482	6,346
percent	54.9%	59.3%	49.5%	61.0%	62.5%	56.6%

SOURCE: U.S. Bureau of the Census, The Hispanic Population in the United States: March, 1985, pp. 14-15, table 2 (data from U.S. Bureau of the Census, *Current Population Reports*). C 3.186:P-20/422
U.S. Bureau of the Census, The Hispanic Population in the United States: March, 1990, pp. 8-9, table 2 (data from U.S. Bureau of the Census, *Current Population Reports*). C 3.186/14-2:990
U.S. Bureau of the Census, "Current Population Reports: The Hispanic Population of the United States, 2000, (Table) 9.1. Labor Force Status of the Civilian Population 16 Years and Over by Sex, Hispanic Origin and Race: March 2000," published March 6, 2001. <http://www..census.gov/population/socdemo/Hispanic/p20-535/tab09-1.txt>

NOTES: 'Other Hispanic origin' includes persons from Spain and persons identifying themselves generally as Hispanic, Spanish, Spanish-American, Hispano, Latino, etc.

UNITS: Total population in thousands of persons 16 years old and over; percent as a percent of total shown (100.0%).

Table 7.04 Civilian Labor Force and Civilian Labor Force Participation
Rates: Projections for 2008

2008	Hispanic	White	Total
civilian labor force			
total	19.6	126.7	154.6
men	11.0	67.7	81.1
women	8.6	59.0	73.4
labor force participation rate			
total	67.7%	67.9%	67.6%
men	77.9	74.5	73.7
women	57.9	61.5	61.9

SOURCE: U.S. Bureau of the Census, Statistical Abstract of the United States, 2000,
p. 403, table 644 (data from U.S. Department of Labor, Bureau of Labor
Statistics) C 3.134:000

NOTES: 'Total' includes other races and ethnic groups not shown separately.

UNITS: Civilian labor force population 16 years old and over in millions of persons;
labor force participation rate as a percent (the civilian noninstitutional
population divided by the civilian labor force).

Table 7.05 Employed Members of the Civilian Labor Force, by Sex and Age, 1985, 1990, 2000

	Hispanic		White		Total	
	male	female	male	female	male	female
1985						
all employed persons 16 years old and over	4,245	2,642	53,046	40,690	59,891	47,259
- persons 16-19 years old	251	187	2,985	2,783	3,328	3,105
- persons 20 years old and over	3,994	2,456	50,061	37,907	56,562	44,154
- persons 65 years old and over	48	27	1,552	978	1,695	1,118
1990						
all employed persons 16 years old and over	5,304	3,504	56,432	45,654	64,435	53,479
- persons 16-19 years old	323	218	2,856	2,662	3,237	3,024
- persons 20 years old and over	4,981	3,286	53,576	42,992	61,198	50,455
- persons 65 years old and over	na	na	1,812	1,288	1,972	1,455
2000						
all employed persons 16 years old and over	8,478	6,014	61,696	51,780	72,293	62,915
- persons 16-19 years old	517	385	3,227	3,043	3,713	3,563
- persons 65 years old and over	130	152	2,130	1,512	2,357	1,713

SOURCE: U.S. Department of Labor, Bureau of Labor Statistics, <u>Handbook of Labor Statistics, 1989</u>, pp. 63-68, table 15, (data from the Current Population Survey). L 2.3/5:989

U.S. Department of Labor, Bureau of Labor Statistics, *Employment and Earnings*, <u>January, 1991</u>, pp. 208, table 39 <u>January, 2001</u>, pp. 168-169, table 3; p. 171, table 4 (data from the Current Population Survey). L 2.41/2:(vol)/1:(year)

NOTES: 'Total' includes other races and ethnic groups not shown separately. Data covers members of the civilian labor force.

UNITS: Employed members of the civilian labor force in thousands of persons, by age group as shown.

Table 7.06   Employed Hispanic Persons as Percent of All Employed Persons in the Civilian Labor Force, by Selected Occupation, 2000

2000

All occupations	10.7%
Managerial and professional specialty	5.0
executive, administrative and managerial	5.4
Professional specialty	4.6
architects	5.5
engineers	3.7
mathematical and computer scientists	3.7
natural scientists	3.2
physicians	3.7
dentists	2.2
health assessment and treatment occupations	3.4
teachers, except college and university	5.2
lawyers and judges	4.1
writers, artists, entertainers, and athletes	5.6
Technicians, sales, and administrative support	8.9
technical and related support	6.9
health technologists	8.2
engineering and related technologists and technicians	6.1
science technicians	8.4
Sales occupations	8.5
Administrative support, including clerical	9.7
computer equipment operators	7.4
secretaries, stenographers, typists	8.6

continued on the next page

Table 7.06   continued

Service occupations	15.7%
private household	31.7
protective service	8.7
fire fighting and fire prevention	5.4
police and detectives	8.4
guards	10.0
Service occupations (except private household and protective service)	16.0
food preparation and service occupations	17.2
health service occupations	10.1
cleaning and building service occupations	23.4
personal service occupations	10.8
Precision production, craft and repair	13.9
mechanics and repairers	10.7
construction trades	16.4
precision production occupations	14.4
Operators, fabricators, and laborers	17.5
machine operators, assemblers, and inspectors	19.3
Transportation and material moving occupations	11.9
Handlers, equipment cleaners, helpers, and laborers	20.7
Farming, forestry, and fishing	23.7
farm operators and managers	3.0

SOURCE: U.S. Department of Labor, Bureau of Labor Statistics, *Employment and Earnings*, January, 2001, pp. 178-183, table 11 (data from the Current Population Survey). L 2.41/2:40/1:001

NOTES: Only selected subcategories of occupational groups displayed.

UNITS: Employed Hispanic persons as a percent of all employed persons, by occupation.

Table 7.07 Employed Hispanic Persons, by Occupation, as Percent of All
Employed Hispanic Persons, by Sex, by Type of Hispanic
Origin, 2000

	Mexican	Puerto Rican	Cuban	Central/ South American	Other Hispanic	Total Hispanic
All employed males						
number	5,542	614	357	1,300	458	8,271
percent	100.0%	100.0%	100.0%	100.0%	100.0%	100.0
by occupation						
executive, administrators,						
managerial	5.2%	6.9%	13.8%	6.7%	11.1%	6.3%
professional specialty	4.0	7.4	8.0	6.0	9.4	5.0
technical and related support	1.2	2.5	4.0	1.9	2.8	1.6
sales	6.7	12.0	15.5	8.8	10.6	8.0
administrative support,						
including clerical	4.8	9.4	6.3	5.8	5.6	5.4
precision production, craft, and						
repair	23.5	17.2	18.3	22.6	15.3	22.2
machine operators, assemblers,						
and inspectors	10.5	10.0	8.5	8.5	8.5	10.0
transportation and material						
moving	6.7	7.7	6.4	10.4	9.3	7.5
handlers, equipment cleaners,						
helpers, and laborers	11.4	9.7	7.1	10.8	8.4	10.9
service workers, private						
household	0.0	0.0	0.0	0.1	0.0	0.0
service workers, except private						
household	14.7	15.9	11.1	15.2	15.9	14.8
farming, forestry, and fishing	11.3	1.2	1.1	3.3	3.2	8.4

Table 7.07   continued

	Mexican	Puerto Rican	Cuban	Central/ South American	Other Hispanic	Total Hispanic
All employed females						
number	3,493	589	262	1,064	450	5,858
percent	100.0%	100.0%	100.0%	100.0%	100.0%	100.0%
by occupation						
executive, administrators, managerial	9.0%	8.7%	12.1%	8.0%	9.8%	9.0%
professional specialty	7.3	11.2	13.7	9.4	13.8	8.9
technical and related support	3.1	3.4	2.6	2.4	3.1	3.0
sales	11.2	13.2	15.1	10.8	12.3	11.6
administrative support, including clerical	23.3	29.9	27.5	18.6	25.3	23.4
precision production, craft, and repair	4.0	2.6	1.3	2.9	1.6	3.3
machine operators, assemblers, and inspectors	10.2	7.8	8.4	10.0	7.2	9.6
transportation and material moving	0.7	0.0	0.0	0.9	1.1	0.7
handlers, equipment cleaners, helpers, and laborers	2.8	2.6	2.6	3.1	2.2	2.8
service workers, private household	3.3	0.9	2.9	9.4	2.0	4.1
service workers, except private household	22.4	19.6	13.9	23.6	21.3	21.9
farming, forestry, and fishing	2.8	0.1	0.0	0.8	0.6	1.9

SOURCE: U.S. Bureau of the Census, "Current Population Reports: The Hispanic Population of the United States, 2000, (Tables) 10.5, 10.6. Detailed Occupation of the Employed Civilian Population 16 Years and Over by Sex, Hispanic Origin and Race: March 2000," published March 6, 2001.
<http: //www..census.gov/population/socdemo/Hispanic/p20-535/tab10-5.txt>
<http: //www..census.gov/population/socdemo/Hispanic/p20-535/tab10-6.txt>

NOTES: Total population includes other races and ethnic groups not shown separately. 'Other Hispanic origin' includes persons from Spain and persons identifying themselves generally as Hispanic, Spanish, Spanish-American, Hispano, Latino, etc.

UNITS: Employed persons in thousands of persons 16 years old and over; percent as a percent of total shown (100.0%).

Table 7.08 Employed Hispanic Persons as Percent of All Employed
Persons in the Civilian Labor Force, by Industry Group, 2000

2000

All industries	10.7%
agriculture	22.5
mining	8.3
construction	14.9
manufacturing	12.3
transportation, communications, and other public utilities	9.4
wholesale and retail trade	12.2
wholesale trade	11.9
retail trade	12.3
finance, insurance and real estate	6.9
services	9.1
public administration	7.3

SOURCE: U.S. Department of Labor, Bureau of Labor Statistics, *Employment and Earnings*, January, 2001; p. 191-194, table 18 (data from Current Population Survey). L 2.41/2:40/1:001

NOTES: Only selected subcategories of industry groups are displayed.

UNITS: Employed Hispanic persons as a percent of all employed persons, by industry group.

Table 7.09 Full-Time and Part-Time Status of the Labor Force, by Region, 1999

	Hispanic	White	Total
1999			
Northeast			
Employed persons			
Full-time workers, total	1,688	17,324	20,373
35 hours of more	1,507	14,981	17,682
at work 1 to 34 hours			
for economic reasons	15	153	174
not at work	51	690	791
Part-time workers, total	271	4,174	4,685
at work for economic reasons	56	338	443
not at work	11	258	285
Unemployed persons			
Looking for full-time work	130	651	906
Looking for part-time work	27	190	244
Midwest			
Employed persons			
Full-time workers, total	946	23,302	26,190
35 hours of more	843	20,326	22,828
at work 1 to 34 hours			
for economic reasons	13	230	267
not at work	33	880	993
Part-time workers, total	147	5,513	6,055
at work for economic reasons	19	329	423
not at work	8	378	406
Unemployed persons			
Looking for full-time work	na	682	917
Looking for part-time work	na	232	280

continued on the next page

Table 7.09   continued

	Hispanic	White	Total
South			
Employed persons			
Full-time workers, total	4,089	31,020	39,435
35 hours of more	3,603	27,203	34,543
at work 1 to 34 hours			
for economic reasons	71	360	480
not at work	125	1,039	1,310
Part-time workers, total	659	5,636	6,971
at work for economic reasons	131	457	687
not at work	28	354	420
Unemployed persons			
Looking for full-time work	229	1,008	1,612
Looking for part-time work	52	249	382
West			
Employed persons			
Full-time workers, total	5,025	20,443	24,198
35 hours of more	4,447	17,828	21,131
at work 1 to 34 hours			
for economic reasons	110	317	359
not at work	156	720	849
Part-time workers, total	873	4,724	5,455
at work for economic reasons	200	551	660
not at work	46	313	349
Unemployed persons			
Looking for full-time work	376	1,007	1,229
Looking for part-time work	67	249	303

SOURCE: U.S. Department of Labor, Bureau of Labor Statistics, Geographic Profile of Employment and Unemployment, 1999, table 2. L 2.3/12:999

NOTES: 'Total' includes other races and ethnic groups not shown separately. The full-time labor force includes persons working part time for economic reasons (slack work; material shortages; repairs to plant or equipment; start or termination of a job during the week; and inability to find full time work).

UNITS: Members of the civilian labor force in thousands of persons, by status, as shown.

Table 7.10 Unemployment Rates for the Civilian Labor Force, by Age, 1985, 1990, 2000

	Hispanic	White	Total
1985			
unemployment rate			
all ages	10.5%	6.2%	7.2%
- persons 16-19 years old	24.3	15.7	18.6
- persons 20 years old and over	9.4	5.5	6.4
- persons 65 years old and over	8.1	2.9	3.2
1990			
unemployment rate			
all ages	8.0%	4.7%	5.5%
- persons 16-19 years old	19.5	13.4	15.5
- persons 25 years old and over	6.8	3.8	4.4
- persons 55 years old and over	6.4	3.4	3.6
2000			
unemployment rate			
all ages	5.7%	3.5%	4.0%
- persons 16-19 years old	16.7	11.4	13.1
- persons 20-24 years old	7.5	5.8	7.1
- persons 25-54 years old	4.4	2.7	3.1
- persons 55-64 years old	4.5	2.4	2.5
- persons 65 years old and over	5.7	2.8	3.1

SOURCE: U.S. Department of Labor, Bureau of Labor Statistics, <u>Handbook of Labor Statistics, 1989</u>, pp. 136-141, table 28, (data from the Current Population Survey). L 2.3/5:989
U.S. Department of Labor, Bureau of Labor Statistics, *Employment and Earnings*, <u>January, 1991</u>; p. 208, table 39; p. 212, table 44; <u>January, 2001</u>; p. 168-169, table 3; p. 171, table 4 (data from the Current Population Survey). L 2.41/2:(vol)/1:(year)

NOTES: 'Total' includes other races and ethnic groups not shown separately. Data covers members of the civilian labor force.

UNITS: Unemployment rate, by age group as shown.

Table 7.11 Unemployment Rates for the Civilian Labor Force, by Sex and Age, 1985, 1990, 2000

	Hispanic		White		Total	
	male	female	male	female	male	female
1985						
unemployment rate						
all ages	10.2	11.0%	6.1%	6.4%	7.0%	7.4%
- persons 16-19 years old	24.7	23.8	16.5	14.8	19.5	17.6
- persons 20 years old						
and over	9.1	9.9	5.4	5.7	6.2	6.6
- persons 65 years old						
and over	9.4	5.5	2.7	3.1	3.1	3.3
1990						
unemployment rate						
all ages	7.8%	8.3%	4.8%	4.6%	5.5%	5.6%
- persons 16-19 years old	19.4	19.6	14.2	12.6	16.3	14.7
- persons 20 years old						
and over	7.0	7.4	4.3	4.1	4.9	4.8
- persons 65 years old						
and over	na	na	2.8	2.8	3.0	3.1
2000						
unemployment rate						
all ages	4.9%	6.7%	3.4%	3.6%	3.9%	4.1%
- persons 16-19 years old	15.7	18.1	12.3	10.4	14.0	12.1
- persons 20-24 years old	6.5	8.9	5.9	5.8	7.3	7.0
- persons 25-54 years old	3.7	5.3	2.5	2.9	2.9	3.3
- persons 55-64 years old	4.1	5.1	2.4	2.4	2.4	2.5
- persons 65 years old						
and over	6.3	4.8	3.1	2.4	3.4	2.8

SOURCE: U.S. Department of Labor, Bureau of Labor Statistics, <u>Handbook of Labor Statistics, 1989</u>, pp. 136-141, table 28, (data from the Current Population Survey). L 2.3/5:989
U.S. Department of Labor, Bureau of Labor Statistics, *Employment and Earnings*, <u>January, 1991</u>; p. 208, table 39; p. 212, table 44; <u>January, 2001</u>; p. 168-169, table 3, p. 171, table 4 (data from the Current Population Survey). L 2.41/2:(vol)/1:(year)

NOTES: 'Total' includes other races and ethnic groups not shown separately. Data covers members of the civilian labor force.

UNITS: Unemployment rate, by age group as shown.

Table 7.12 Unemployment Rates for the Hispanic Civilian Labor Force, by Sex, and Type of Hispanic Origin, 1985, 1990, 2000

	Mexican	Puerto Rican	Cuban	Central/ South American	Other Hispanic	Total Hispanic
1985						
Unemployment rate						
both sexes	11.9%	14.3%	6.8	11.0%	7.1%	11.3%
males	12.5	15.0	6.9	9.3	8.9	11.8
females	10.9	13.3	6.6	13.2	4.9	10.5
1990						
Unemployment rate						
both sexes	9.0%	8.6%	5.8%	6.6%	6.2%	8.2%
males	8.6	8.2	6.3	6.9	6.2	8.0
females	9.8	9.1	5.1	6.3	5.9	8.5
2000						
Unemployment rate						
both sexes	7.0%	8.1%	5.8%	5.1%	7.8%	6.8%
males	6.1	8.0	6.7	4.5	8.8	6.2
females	8.5	8.3	4.6	5.9	6.7	7.7

SOURCE: U.S. Bureau of the Census, The Hispanic Population in the United States: March, 1985, pp. 14-15, table 2 (data from U.S. Bureau of the Census, *Current Population Reports*). C 3.186:P-20/422

U.S. Bureau of the Census, The Hispanic Population in the United States:, March, 1990, pp. 8-9, table 2; March, 1992, pp. 14-15, table 2 (data from U.S. Bureau of the Census, *Current Population Reports*). C 3.186/14-2:(year)

U.S. Bureau of the Census, "Current Population Reports: The Hispanic Population of the United States, 2000, (Table) 9.2. Employment Status of the Population 16 Years and Over in the Civilian Labor Force by Sex, Hispanic Origin and Race: March 2000," published March 6, 2001. <http://www..census.gov/population/socdemo/Hispanic/p20-535/tab09-2.txt>

NOTES: Total population includes other races and ethnic groups not shown separately. 'Other Hispanic origin' includes persons from Spain and persons identifying themselves generally as Hispanic, Spanish, Spanish-American, Hispano, Latino, etc.

UNITS: Total population in thousands of persons 16 years old and over; percent as a percent of total shown (100.0%).

Table 7.13 Unemployment by Reason for Unemployment, by Region, 1990 and 1999

	Hispanic	White	Total
1990			
Northeast			
job losers	56.7%	56.7%	55.7%
job leavers	9.9	12.1	12.3
re-entrants to the labor force	22.0	23.3	23.7
new entrants to the labor force	11.4	7.8	8.2
Midwest			
job losers	54.2%	52.5%	50.7%
job leavers	9.4	14.7	13.8
re-entrants to the labor force	27.3	25.6	26.8
new entrants to the labor force	9.0	7.2	8.8
South			
job losers	47.6%	44.0%	43.3%
job leavers	16.7	18.0	16.1
re-entrants to the labor force	23.4	28.2	29.2
new entrants to the labor force	12.4	9.8	11.4
West			
job losers	55.5%	47.8%	46.7%
job leavers	12.5	16.2	16.0
re-entrants to the labor force	20.0	27.9	28.7
new entrants to the labor force	12.1	8.1	8.5

continued on the next page

Table 7.13   continued

	Hispanic	White	Total
1999			
Northeast			
job losers	45.6%	50.1%	48.4%
job leavers	8.9	12.7	11.7
re-entrants to the labor force	36.1	30.6	32.3
new entrants to the labor force	8.9	6.5	7.7
Midwest			
job losers	na%	47.0%	45.2%
job leavers	na	14.7	13.6
re-entrants to the labor force	na	31.8	34.6
new entrants to the labor force	na	6.3	6.5
South			
job losers	41.3%	41.7%	40.9%
job leavers	12.5	17.2	14.9
re-entrants to the labor force	34.9	33.1	35.0
new entrants to the labor force	11.7	8.0	9.1
West			
job losers	51.2%	47.0%	46.1%
job leavers	7.9	12.7	12.1
re-entrants to the labor force	32.3	33.4	33.9
new entrants to the labor force	8.8	7.1	7.9

SOURCE: U.S. Department of Labor, Bureau of Labor Statistics, Geographic Profile of Employment and Unemployment, 1990, pp. 29-30, table 10; 1999, table 10. L 2.3/12:(year)

NOTES: 'Total' includes other races and ethnic groups not shown separately. Data covers members of the civilian labor force.

UNITS: Unemployed members of the civilian labor force in thousands of persons, by reason for unemployment as shown.

Table 7.14   Duration of Unemployment, by Region of Residence, 1992 and 1999

	Hispanic	White	Total
1992			
Northeast			
less than 5 weeks	26.6%	25.9%	25.5%
5-14 weeks	28.0	27.9	27.8
15 weeks and over	45.4	46.1	46.7
27 weeks and over	26.0	28.0	28.5
52 weeks and over	15.1	14.5	15.5
Midwest			
less than 5 weeks	36.9%	36.2%	37.0%
5-14 weeks	32.4	30.4	30.5
15 weeks and over	30.7	33.4	32.5
27 weeks and over	16.8	18.5	18.2
52 weeks and over	8.8	10.0	10.2
South			
less than 5 weeks	43.6%	38.7%	38.0%
5-14 weeks	27.9	29.7	29.6
15 weeks and over	28.5	31.7	32.4
27 weeks and over	15.4	18.1	18.4
52 weeks and over	6.8	9.4	10.1
West			
less than 5 weeks	40.3%	38.3%	37.3%
5-14 weeks	28.4	29.0	29.7
15 weeks and over	31.3	32.7	33.0
27 weeks and over	17.2	18.1	18.4
52 weeks and over	9.5	9.4	9.6

continued on the next page

Table 7.14   continued

	Hispanic	White	Total
1999			
Northeast			
less than 5 weeks	33.5%	40.6%	37.8%
5-14 weeks	27.8	31.1	30.7
15 weeks and over	38.0	28.3	31.5
27 weeks and over	20.9	13.2	15.8
52 weeks and over	12.7	7.1	8.5
Midwest			
less than 5 weeks	na%	49.7%	47.2%
5-14 weeks	na	31.0	30.9
15 weeks and over	na	19.4	21.9
27 weeks and over	na	8.6	9.9
52 weeks and over	na	4.9	5.7
South			
less than 5 weeks	50.2%	48.2%	44.6%
5-14 weeks	29.2	31.0	31.7
15 weeks and over	20.6	20.8	23.6
27 weeks and over	8.9	9.5	11.6
52 weeks and over	6.0	5.1	6.6
West			
less than 5 weeks	46.3%	45.7%	44.0%
5-14 weeks	32.5	30.8	30.9
15 weeks and over	21.2	23.5	25.0
27 weeks and over	9.0	11.4	12.5
52 weeks and over	4.5	5.8	6.7

SOURCE: U.S. Department of Labor, Bureau of Labor Statistics, <u>Geographic Profile of Employment and Unemployment, 1992</u>, pp. 33-34, table 11, <u>1999</u>, table 11. L 2.3/12:(year)

NOTES: 'Total' includes other races and ethnic groups not shown separately.

UNITS: Duration of unemployment by region as a percent of total unemployment in each region, 100.0%.

Table 7.15   Workers Paid Hourly Rates With Earnings at or Below the
Minimum Wage, 2000

	Hispanic	White	Total
Number of workers			
All workers paid hourly rates	9,847	59,374	72,744
at or below $5.15 per hour	318	2,242	2,710
at $5.15 per hour	129	687	866
below $5.15 per hour	189	1,555	1,844
Percent of all workers **paid hourly rates**			
All at or below $5.15 per hour	3.2%	3.8%	3.7%
at $5.15 per hour	1.3	1.2	1.2
below $5.15 per hour	1.9	2.6	2.5
Median hourly earnings	$8.50	$9.98	$9.91

SOURCE: U.S. Bureau of the Census, <u>Statistical Abstract of the United States, 2001</u>;
              p. 405, table 625 (data from the U.S. Bureau of Labor Statistics).
              C3.134:001

NOTES: 'Total' includes other races/ethnic groups not shown separately.
              Workers 16 years and over.

UNITS: Number of workers in thousands; 'percent of all workers paid hourly rates'
              in percent, as a percent of total, 100.0%; median hourly earnings of
              workers paid hourly rates in dollars per hour.

Table 7.16   Union Membership, by Sex, 2000

	Hispanic	White	Total
Men			
total employed	7,884	53,105	62,853
members of unions			
number	972	7,911	9,578
as a percent of total			
employed	12.3%	14.9%	15.2%
represented by unions			
total	1,063	8,541	10,355
as a percent of total			
employed	13.5%	16.1%	16.5%
Women			
total employed	5,725	47,350	57,933
members of unions			
number	582	5,183	6,680
as a percent of total			
employed	10.2%	10.9%	11.5%
represented by unions			
total	677	5,912	7,590
as a percent of total			
employed	11.8%	12.5%	13.1%

SOURCE: U.S. Department of Labor, Bureau of Labor Statistics, *Employment and Earnings*, January 2001; p. 218, table 40, (data from the Current Population Survey). L 2.41/2:40/1:001

NOTES: 'Total' includes other races/ethnic groups not shown separately. 'Members of unions' includes members of a labor union or an employee association similar to a union. 'Represented by unions' includes members of a labor union or an employee association similar to a union as well as workers who report no union affiliation but whose jobs are covered by a union or an employee association contract.

UNITS: Total employed, members of unions and represented by unions in thousands of persons 16 years old and older; percent as shown.

Table 7.17   Educational Attainment of Persons 16 Years and Over, by
Labor Force Status and Sex, 2000

	Hispanic		White		Total	
	male	female	male	female	male	female
High school graduate						
Employed	2,446	1,739	16,710	14,588	22,377	19,681
Unemployed	140	110	697	535	1,136	951
Not in labor force	415	1,106	5,577	11,677	7,173	14,757
Bachelor's degree						
Employed	551	510	10,789	9,363	13,028	11,786
Unemployed	19	20	171	172	250	225
Not in labor force	66	161	1,896	3,292	2,248	4,032

SOURCE: U.S. Bureau of the Census, <u>Current Population Reports: Educational
Attainment in the United States: March 2000 (Update)</u>, Series P-20,
#536, pp. 1-7, 11, 12, table 5a. <www.census.gov>

NOTES: 'Total' includes other races and ethnic groups not shown separately. 'White'
does not include persons of Hispanic origin.

UNITS: Number of persons in thousands.

Table 7.18 Unemployment Rates of the Civilian Labor Force 25 - 64 Years of Age, by Educational Attainment, 1992 - 2000

	Hispanic	White	Total
1992			
Total	9.8%	6.0%	6.7%
less than a high school diploma	13.6	12.9	13.5
high school graduate, no college	9.6	6.8	7.7
less than a bachelor's degree	5.9	5.3	5.9
college graduate	4.2	2.7	2.9
1993			
Total	10.3%	5.8%	6.4%
less than a high school diploma	14.5	12.4	13.0
high school graduate, no college	9.1	6.5	7.3
less than a bachelor's degree	7.0	5.0	5.5
college graduate	5.2	3.1	3.2
1994			
Total	9.7%	5.2%	5.8%
less than a high school diploma	13.4	11.7	12.6
high school graduate, no college	8.3	5.8	6.7
less than a bachelor's degree	7.2	4.5	5.0
college graduate	5.2	2.6	2.9
2000			
Total	5.5%	3.0%	3.3
less than a high school diploma	8.3	7.5	7.9
high school graduate, no college	4.6	3.3	3.8
less than a bachelor's degree	3.1	2.7	3.0
college graduate	3.2	1.4	1.5

SOURCE: U.S. Bureau of the Census, Statistical Abstract of the United States, 1999; p. 432, table 684; 2001; p. 389, table 604 (data from U.S. Department of Labor, Bureau of Labor Statistics). C 3.134(year)

NOTES: 'Total' includes other races/ethnic groups not shown separately. Data is for persons 25 years old and over.

UNITS: Unemployment rates (percent of the civilian labor force that is unemployed) as a percent of the total civilian labor force.

Table 7.19 Self-employed Persons, 1997

	Hispanic	White	Total
1997			
worked at home	156	3,868	4,125
percent who worked less than 8 hours	27.8%	30.5%	30.4%
8 hours or more			
total	72.2	69.5	69.6
35 hours or more	31.3	29.0	29.3
mean hours:			
worked at home	23.8	22.9	23.0
total at work on primary job	35.9	36.9	37.3

SOURCE: U.S. Department of Labor, Bureau of Labor Statistics, "Table 5: Home-based businesses: Self-employed persons by selected characteristics, May 1997;" pp. 1-2, table 5. <http://stats.bls.gov/news.release/homey.t05.htm> accesses 19 November, 1998.

NOTES: Data refer to employed persons in nonagricultural industries who reported work in a home-based business during the survey reference week as part of their primary job. Detail for the above race and Hispanic-origin groups will not sum to totals because data for the "other races" group are not presented and Hispanics are included in both the white and black population groups. Data reflect revised population controls used in the Current Population Survey effective with January 1997 estimates.

UNITS: Numbers in thousands of persons. Percent as a percent of persons working at home.

Table 7.20   Unemployment, by Reason for Unemployment, 1994 - 2000

	Hispanic	White	Total
1994			
Total	1,187	5,892	7,996
job losers	573	2,972	3,815
job leavers	89	638	791
re-entrants to the labor force	402	1,898	2,786
new entrants to the labor force	124	385	604
2000			
Total	876	4,099	5,655
job losers	390	1,866	2,492
job leavers	98	593	775
re-entrants to the labor force	289	1,356	1,957
new entrants to the labor force	99	284	431

SOURCE: U.S. Department of Labor, Bureau of Labor Statistics, *Employment and Earnings*, January, 1996; p. 196, table 28; January, 2001; p. 203, table 28 (data from the Current Population Survey). L2.41/2:(vol)/1:(year)

NOTES: 'Total' includes other races and ethnic groups not shown separately. Data covers members of the civilian labor force.

UNITS: Unemployed members of the civilian labor force in thousands of persons, by reason for unemployment as shown.

Table 7.21   Self-Employed Workers, 1994 - 2000

	Hispanic	White	Total
1994	533	8,179	9,003
1995	507	8,105	8,902
1996	561	8,106	8,971
1997	598	8,153	9,056
1998	590	8,030	8,962
1999	651	7,846	8,790
2000	616	7,692	8,674

SOURCE: U.S. Department of Labor, Bureau of Labor Statistics, *Employment and Earnings*, January, 1994; p. 230, table 41; January, 1999; p. 184, table 12; January, 2000; p. 184, table 12; January, 2001; p. 184, table 12 (data from the Current Population Survey). L2.41/2:(vol)/1:(year)

NOTES: 'Total' includes other races and ethnic groups not shown separately.

UNITS: Self-employed workers in thousands of persons.

Table 7.22 Employment Status of Families, 2000

	Hispanic	White	Total
Total families	7,581	59,918	71,680
With employed member(s)	6,633	49,877	59,626
Some usually work full time	6,255	46,639	55,683
With no employed member	947	10,042	12,054
With unemployed member(s)	679	3,010	4,110
Some member(s) employed	493	2,276	2,973
Some usually work full time	446	2,052	2,675

SOURCE: U.S. Department Labor, Bureau Labor Statistics; "Employment Characteristics of Families, 2000 (Table) 1. Employment and unemployment in families, by race and Hispanic origin, 1999-2000 annual averages"; <http://stats.bls.gov/news.release/famee.t0l.htm> (accessed: 22 November 2001)

NOTES: 'Total' includes other races and ethnic groups not shown separately.

UNITS: Number of families in thousands of families.

Chapter 8: Earnings, Income, Poverty & Wealth

Table 8.01   Money Income of Households, 1980 - 2000

	Hispanic	White	Total
Median income			
1980	$24,582	$33,645	$31,891
1985	24,055	34,306	32,530
1987	25,225	35,821	33,999
1988	25,505	36,055	34,106
1989	26,199	36,340	34,547
1990	25,320	35,413	33,952
1991	24,690	34,350	32,780
1992	23,869	34,023	32,361
1993	23,472	33,804	32,041
1994	23,421	34,028	32,264
1996	24,906	37,161	35,492
1997	26,628	38,972	37,005
1998	28,330	40,912	38,885
1999	30,735	42,504	40,816
2000	33,447	44,226	42,148
Mean income			
1980	$30,025	$39,459	$37,929
1985	30,057	41,676	40,033
1987	32,335	44,088	42,281
1988	32,563	44,432	42,615
1989	33,455	45,465	43,647
1990	31,717	44,122	42,411
1991	31,416	43,005	41,263
1992	30,445	42,880	41,027
1993	31,067	44,393	42,489
1994	31,582	45,034	43,133
1996	34,005	48,994	47,123
1997	35,883	51,902	49,692
1998	38,280	54,207	51,855
1999	40,452	56,908	54,842
2000	42,410	59,277	57,045

SOURCE: U.S. Bureau of the Census, Current Population Reports: Income, Poverty, and Valuation of Noncash Benefits: 1994, Series P-60, #189, pp. B-2 - B-3, table B-1. C3.186/2:994
U.S. Bureau of the Census, Current Population Reports: Money Income in the United States: 1996, Series P-60, #197; p. 5, table 2 C3.186/2:996; 1997, Series P-60, #200; p. 5, table 2; 1998, Series P-60, #206; p. 5, table 2; 1999, Series P-60, #209; p. 6, table 2.
U.S. Bureau of the Census, "Current Population Reports: Income 2000, (Table) 2. Selected Characteristics – Households by Total Money Income in 2000;" published 20 September 2001; <http://www.census.gov/hhes/income/income00/inctab2.html>

NOTES: 'Total' includes other races and ethnic groups not shown separately.

UNITS: Median and mean money income in 1994 CPI-U-XI adjusted dollars, as shown.

Table 8.02   Money Income of Households, by Selected Household
Characteristic, 2000

	Hispanic	White	Total
2000			
Number of households	9,663	88,545	106,417
number of households with			
current dollar incomes of:			
under $5,000	320	2,066	3,064
$5,000-$9,999	702	4,888	6,479
10,000-$14,999	798	5,868	7,412
$15,000-$24,999	1,765	11,523	14,270
$25,000-$34,999	1,422	11,120	13,313
$35,000-$49,999	1,706	13,594	16,468
$50,000-$74,999	1,682	17,192	20,099
$75,000-$99,999	711	9,712	11,050
$100,000 and over	556	12,582	14,262
median income	$33,447	$44,226	$42,148
mean income	$42,410	$59,277	$57,045
Median income by:			
type of residence			
inside metropolitan area	$34,345	$47,353	$44,984
outside metropolitan area	26,067	34,150	32,837
type of household			
family households	$36,575	$54,292	$51,751
married couple families	41,117	60,081	59,346
non-family households	21,255	25,983	25,438
male householder living alone	20,589	27,324	26,720
female householder living alone	13,296	18,695	18,163
age of householder			
15-24 years old	$27,850	$29,394	$27,689
25-34 years old	34,096	47,021	44,473
35-44 years old	38,058	56,498	53,240
45-54 years old	41,107	61,679	58,218
55-64 years old	32,179	47,073	44,992
65 years old and over	17,256	23,620	23,048

continued on the next page

Table 8.02 continued

	Hispanic	White	Total
2000 - continued			
size of household			
one person	$16,220	$21,968	$21,467
two persons	30,357	46,248	44,526
three persons	35,163	58,035	54,199
four persons	40,468	64,664	61,852
five persons	38,768	62,130	60,293
six persons	40,361	56,913	54,293
seven or more persons	45,758	57,432	54,659
number of earners			
no earners	$ 9,893	$16,577	$15,168
one earner	23,649	35,387	33,398
two earners or more	48,418	67,480	66,068
work experience of the householder			
all civilian householders	$33,447	$44,226	42,148
worked	38,834	54,574	52,146
worked year-round full-time	42,765	59,717	57,149
did not work	17,436	22,122	20,819

SOURCE: U.S. Bureau of the Census, "Current Population Reports: Income 2000, (Table) 1. Median Income of Households by Selected Characteristics, Race, and Hispanic Origin of Householder: 2000, 1999, and 1998;" published 20 September 2001; <http://www.census.gov/hhes/income/income00/inctab1.html>
U.S. Bureau of the Census, "Current Population Reports: Income 2000, (Table) 2. Selected Characteristics – Households by Total Money Income in 2000;" published 20 September 2001; <http://www.census.gov/hhes/income/income00/inctab2.html>

NOTES: 'Total' includes other races and ethnic groups not shown separately. Number of households as of March of the following year. 'Occupation of the householder' represents the longest job held by the householder.

UNITS: Number of households in thousands; mean and median income in current dollars.

Table 8.03 Money Income of Households by Type of Hispanic
Origin, 2000

	Mexican	Puerto Rican	Cuban	Central/ South American	Other Hispanic	Total Hispanic
All households	100.0%	100.0%	100.0%	100.0%	100.0%	100.0%
percent with incomes of:						
$1 to $2,499 or loss	1.8	3.7	1.6	2.9	2.9	2.3
$2,500 to $4,999	1.6	2.7	2.5	1.2	1.4	1.7
$5,000 to $9,999	7.1	12.5	12.8	5.8	8.9	8.0
$10,000 to $14,999	10.1	8.9	12.0	7.9	9.1	9.7
$15,000 to $19,999	10.5	9.7	6.7	8.6	8.6	9.8
$20,000 to $24,999	9.7	7.9	6.7	8.6	8.3	9.1
$25,000 to $34,999	16.1	12.9	13.1	18.0	14.7	15.8
$35,000 to $49.999	16.7	17.1	12.2	18.3	15.9	16.7
$50,000 to $74,999	15.9	13.6	13.3	13.7	15.4	15.2
$75,000 and over	10.4	10.9	19.1	14.9	14.7	12.0

SOURCE: U.S. Bureau of the Census, "Current Population Reports: The Hispanic
            Population of the United States, 2000, (Table) 12.1. Total Money
            Income in 1999 of Households by Type, Hispanic Origin and Race of
            Householder: March 2000," published March 6, 2001.
            <http: //www..census.gov/population/socdemo/Hispanic/p20-535/tab12-1.txt>

NOTES: Total population includes other races and ethnic groups not shown
            separately. 'Other Hispanic origin' includes persons from Spain and
            persons identifying themselves generally as Hispanic, Spanish, Spanish-
            American, Hispano, Latino, etc.

UNITS: Percent as a percent of total shown (100.0%).

Table 8.04 Money Income of Families, 1980 - 2000

	Hispanic	White	Total
Median income			
1980	$29,281	$43,583	$41,830
1985	29,200	44,739	42,564
1987	29,605	47,230	45,166
1989	31,616	48,511	46,135
1990	30,085	47,398	45,392
1991	29,596	46,798	44,514
1992	28,421	46,659	44,129
1993	27,822	46,226	43,472
1994	27,990	47,058	44,638
1995	27,588	47,884	45,599
1996	28,618	48,925	46,240
1997	30,111	50,026	47,687
1998	31,243	51,729	49,317
1999	32,727	52,945	50,594
2000	35,050	53,256	50,891
Mean income			
1980	$35,049	$49,622	$47,702
1985	35,531	52,754	50,558
1987	37,699	56,190	53,791
1989	39,371	58,528	55,970
1990	37,634	57,178	54,764
1991	37,155	56,076	53,553
1992	36,169	56,026	53,357
1993	36,591	58,302	55,542
1994	37,234	59,517	56,791
1995	36,665	60,179	57,661
1996	38,908	61,432	58,676
1997	40,427	63,757	60,884
1998	41,920	65,828	62,879
1999	43,297	67,406	64,740
2000	44,185	68,310	65,574

SOURCE: U.S. Bureau of the Census, "Current Population Reports: Historical Income Tables - Families, (Table) F-23. Families by Total Money Income, Race, and Hispanic Origin of Householder: 1967 to 2000;" published 20 September 2001; <http://www.census.gov/hhes/income/histinc/f23.html>

NOTES: 'Total' includes other races and ethnic groups not shown separately.

UNITS: Median and mean money income in 2000 CPI-U-RS 28/ adjusted dollars, as shown.

Table 8.05 Money Income of Families, by Selected Family Characteristic, 1985

	Hispanic	White	Total
Families			
Number of families	4,206	54,991	63,558
percent of families with incomes:			
under $2,500	2.9%	1.6%	1.9%
$2,500-$4,499	5.4	2.1	2.9
$5,000-$7,499	8.5	3.6	4.2
$7,500-$9,999	8.5	3.9	4.3
$10,000-$12,499	8.1	4.8	5.2
$12,500-$14,999	6.8	4.9	5.0
$15,000-$19,999	12.1	10.3	10.5
$20,000-$24,999	11.3	10.4	10.3
$25,000-$34,999	16.0	19.2	18.6
$35,000-$49,999	12.5	19.7	18.8
$50,000 and over	8.1	19.6	18.3
median income	$19,027	$29,152	$27,735
mean income	$23,152	$34,375	$32,944
Median family income by:			
type of family			
married couple families	$22,269	$31,602	$31,100
wife in paid labor force	28,132	36,992	36,431
wife not in paid labor force	17,116	25,307	24,556
male householder,			
no wife present	19,773	24,190	22,622
female householder,			
no husband present	8,792	15,825	13,660

continued on the next page

Table 8.05 continued

	Hispanic	White	Total
Mean family income by:			
type of income			
wages and salaries	$22,566	$31,277	$30,258
non-farm self-employment	14,628	14,565	14,420
farm self employment	na	4,593	4,557
property income	1,483	3,486	3,327
- interest income	1,017	2,440	2,328
transfer payments and all other income	5,347	7,776	7,469
- social security or railroad retirement income	6,014	7,684	7,488
-public assistance and supplemental income	4,458	3,416	3,498

SOURCE: U.S. Bureau of the Census, Current Population Reports: Money Income of Households Families and Persons in the United States; March 1985, Series P-60, #156, pp. 26-29, tables 9, 10; pp. 40-46, tables 13, 14; pp. 56-64, table 17; pp. 86-88, table 25. C3.186:P-60/156
U.S. Bureau of the Census, Statistical Abstract of the United States, 1987, p. 437, table 734, (data from *the Current Population Survey*). C 3.134:987

NOTES: 'Total' includes other races and ethnic groups not shown separately. Number of families as of March of the following year. 'Occupation of the householder' represents the longest job held by the householder. 'Property income' includes interest, dividends, net rental income, income from trusts and estates, and net royalty income.

UNITS: Number of families and families with income, in thousands of families; percent as a percent as shown; mean income in current dollars.

Table 8.06 Money Income of Families, by Selected Family Characteristic, 1990

	Hispanic	White	Total
Families			
Number of families	4,981	58,803	66,322
percent of families with current dollar incomes of:			
under $5,000	6.3%	2.5%	3.6%
$5,000-$9,999	12.3	4.7	5.8
$10,000-$14,999	12.6	7.0	7.5
$15,000-$24,999	21.7	16.0	16.4
$25,000-$34,999	16.6	16.5	16.2
$35,000-$49,999	15.7	20.8	20.0
$50,000-$74,999	10.0	19.3	18.2
$75,000-$99,999	2.9	7.3	6.9
$100,000 and over	1.9	5.9	5.4
mean income	$29,311	$44,532	$42,652
median income	$23,341	$36,915	$35,353
Median income by:			
type of residence			
nonfarm	$23,402	$36,974	$35,376
farm	na	34,476	34,171
inside metropolitan area	23,898	40,086	37,893
outside metropolitan area	19,061	29,693	28,272
type of family			
married couple families	$27,996	$40,331	$39,895
wife in paid labor force	34,778	47,247	46,777
wife not in paid labor force	21,168	30,781	30,265
male householder, no wife present	21,744	30,570	29,046
female householder, no husband present	11,914	19,528	16,932

continued on the next page

Table 8.06 continued

	Hispanic	White	Total
Median income by:			
age of householder			
15-24 years old	$13,009	$18,234	$16,219
25-34 years old	20,439	33,457	31,497
35-44 years old	27,350	42,632	41,061
45-54 years old	29,908	49,249	47,165
55-64 years old	30,839	40,416	39,035
65 years old and over	17,962	25,864	25,049
size of family			
two persons	$19,230	$31,734	$30,428
three persons	22,778	38,858	36,644
four persons	25,808	43,352	41,451
five persons	25,727	41,037	39,452
six persons	24,786	40,387	38,379
seven or more persons	30,549	39,845	35,363
number of earners			
no earners	$ 8,858	$17,369	$15,047
one earner	16,795	27,670	25,878
two earners or more	33,704	46,261	45,462

SOURCE: U.S. Bureau of the Census, Current Population Reports: Money Income of Households, Families, and Persons in the United States: March 1990, Series P-60, #174, pp. 52-55, table 13; p. 56, table 14. C3.186/2:990

NOTES: 'Total' includes other races and ethnic groups not shown separately. Number of families as of March of the following year.

UNITS: Number of families and families with income, in thousands of families; percent as a percent as shown; mean and median income in current dollars.

Table 8.07 Money Income of Families, by Selected Family Characteristic, 2000

	Hispanic	White	Total
Families			
Number of families	7,728	60,218	72,383
with current dollar incomes of:			
under $5,000	276	1,020	1,569
$5,000-$9,999	376	1,388	2,067
$10,000-$14,999	607	2,382	3,277
$15,000-$24,999	1,411	6,455	8,308
$25,000-$34,999	1,187	7,118	8,701
$35,000-$49,999	1,398	9,602	11,519
$50,000-$74,999	1,385	13,371	15,543
$75,000-$99,999	617	8,073	9,118
$100,000 and over	471	10,809	12,282
median income	$35,050	$53,256	$50,891
mean income	$44,185	$68,310	$65,574
Median income by:			
type of residence			
inside metropolitan area	$35,564	$57,221	$54,058
outside metropolitan area	29,002	42,587	41,104
type of family			
married couple families	$40,631	$59,953	$59,187
wife in paid labor force	50,448	70,462	69,467
wife not in paid labor force	28,675	40,145	39,738
male householder, no wife present	32,852	39,427	37,523
female householder,			
no husband present	21,006	28,371	25,787

continued on the next page

Table 8.07   continued

	Hispanic	White	Total
Median income by:			
age of householder			
15-24 years old	$27,725	$29,293	$26,508
25-34 years old	31,987	49,054	45,890
35-44 years old	37,372	61,099	58,086
45-54 years old	42,912	70,706	68,084
55-64 years old	38,451	57,978	55,717
65 years old and over	24,330	33,467	32,854
size of family			
two persons	$27,958	$44,317	$42,259
three persons	32,974	57,018	52,883
four persons	38,376	65,382	62,233
five persons	38,590	62,424	60,704
six persons	40,179	57,115	55,076
seven or more persons	45,609	56,236	53,850
number of earners			
no earners	$12,274	$23,759	$21,913
one earner	22,734	37,187	34,424
two earners or more	48,533	68,969	67,602

SOURCE: U.S. Bureau of the Census, "Current Population Reports: Income 2000, (Table) 4. Median Income of Families by Selected Characteristics, Race, and Hispanic Origin of Householder: 2000, 1999, and 1998;" published 20 September 2001; <http://www.census.gov/hhes/income/income00/inctab4.html>
U.S. Bureau of the Census, "Current Population Reports: Income 2000, (Table) 5. Selected Characteristics of families by Total Money Income in 2000;" published 20 September 2001; <http://www.census.gov/hhes/income/income00/inctab5.html>

NOTES: 'Total' includes other races and ethnic groups not shown separately. Number of families as of March of the following year.

UNITS: Number of families and families with income, in thousands of families; mean and median income in current dollars.

Table 8.08   Money Income of Families, by Type of Hispanic Origin, 2000

	Mexican	Puerto Rican	Cuban	Central/ South American	Other Hispanic	Total Hispanic
All families	100.0%	100.0%	100.0%	100.0%	100.0%	100.0%
percent with incomes of:						
$1 to $2,499 or loss	2.1	3.3	1.8	3.0	2.2	2.3
$2,500 to $4,999	1.8	3.6	1.8	1.3	1.9	1.9
$5,000 to $9,999	5.6	8.6	4.6	4.5	6.2	5.7
$10,000 to $14,999	8.9	9.4	11.2	7.7	9.5	8.9
$15,000 to $19,999	10.8	11.3	7.1	9.4	9.0	10.3
$20,000 to $24,999	10.1	7.4	6.3	9.2	7.9	9.4
$25,000 to $34,999	16.2	13.2	15.6	17.9	13.3	15.9
$35,000 to $49.999	16.8	17.4	12.0	17.0	17.6	16.7
$50,000 to $74,999	16.9	13.7	16.7	13.8	14.7	15.9
$75,000 and over	10.9	12.3	22.9	16.2	17.7	12.8

SOURCE: U.S. Bureau of the Census, "Current Population Reports: The Hispanic Population of the United States, 2000, (Table) 13.1. Total Money Income in 1999 of Families by Type, Hispanic Origin and Race of Householder: March 2000," published March 6, 2001.
<http://www..census.gov/population/socdemo/Hispanic/p20-535/tab13-1.txt>

NOTES: 'Other Hispanic origin' includes persons from Spain and persons identifying themselves generally as Hispanic, Spanish, Spanish-American, Hispano, Latino, etc. Income from the previous year.

UNITS: Percent as a percent of total shown (100.0%)

Table 8.09 Median Weekly Earnings of Families, by Type of Family and Number of Earners, 1985, 1990, 1993

	Hispanic	White	Total
1985			
All families with earners	na	$543	$522
married couple families	na	589	582
with one earner	na	395	385
with two or more earners	na	723	715
families maintained by women	na	311	297
families maintained by men	na	475	450
1990			
All families with earners	$496	$681	$653
married couple families	555	745	732
with one earner	322	473	455
with two or more earners	716	892	880
families maintained by women	326	382	363
families maintained by men	468	539	514
1993			
All families with earners	$505	$739	$707
married couple families	566	816	804
with one earner	334	492	481
with two or more earners	744	984	973
families maintained by women	353	415	393
families maintained by men	432	547	523

SOURCE: U.S. Department of Labor, Bureau of Labor Statistics, Handbook of Labor Statistics, 1989; p. 200, table 44 (data from the Current Population Survey). L 2.3/5:989
U.S. Department of Labor, Bureau of Labor Statistics, *Employment and Earnings*, January, 1991; p. 219, table 52; January, 1994; p. 239, table 52 (data from the Current Population Survey). L 2.41/2:37/1:(year)

NOTES: 'Total' includes other races and ethnic groups not shown separately. Data excludes families in which there is no wage or salary earner, or in which the husband, wife, or other person maintaining the family is either self-employed or in the armed forces.

UNITS: Median weekly earnings in dollars.

Table 8.10   Median Income of Year-Round, Full-Time Workers, by Sex, 1980 - 2000

	Hispanic		White		Total	
	male	female	male	female	male	female
1980	$23,113	$16,500	$32,658	$19,224	$31,729	$19,088
1981	22,921	16,707	32,243	18,854	31,548	18,687
1982	22,574	16,308	31,703	19,313	30,932	19,099
1983	22,776	16,430	31,577	19,814	30,822	19,601
1984	22,875	16,940	32,357	20,125	31,352	19,958
1985	22,233	17,037	32,678	20,596	31,548	20,372
1986	21,525	17,712	33,189	21,022	32,330	20,779
1987	21,532	17,939	32,764	21,088	32,044	20,886
1988	21,171	17,606	32,292	21,133	31,613	20,880
1989	20,771	17,721	32,293	21,409	30,924	21,236
1990	20,542	16,823	31,002	21,521	29,711	21,278
1991	20,366	16,733	31,177	21,420	30,307	21,172
1992	20,049	17,138	31,012	21,659	30,358	21,440
1993	20,423	17,112	31,832	22,979	31,077	22,469
1994	20,525	18,418	32,440	23,894	31,612	23,265
1995	20,553	17,855	33,515	24,264	32,199	23,777
1996	21,265	19,272	34,741	25,358	33,538	24,935
1997	21,799	19,676	36,118	26,470	35,248	26,029
1998	22,505	19,817	37,196	27,304	36,252	26,855
1999	23,342	20,052	39,331	28,023	37,574	27,370
2000	25,041	21,026	40,350	29,659	39,020	28,823

SOURCE: U.S. Bureau of the Census, Current Population Reports: Money Income of Households, Families, and Persons in the United States: March 1992, Series P-60, #184; p. B 36, table B-17; 1996, Series P-60, #197, pp.28-29, table 7. C3.186/2:(year)

U.S. Bureau of the Census, Current Population Reports: Income Poverty, and Valuation of Noncash Benefits: 1994, Series P-60, #189, pp. 15-16, table 5. C3.186/2:994

U.S. Bureau of the Census, Current Population Reports: Money Income in the United States: 1999, Series P-60, #209, pp. 30-31, table 7.<www.census.gov>

U.S. Bureau of the Census, "Current Population Reports: Income 2000, (Table) 7. Median Income of People by Selected Characteristics: 2000, 1999, and 1998;" published 20 September 2001; <http://www.census.gov/hhes/income/income00/inctab7.html>

NOTES: 'Total' includes other races/ethnic groups not shown separately. Data covers the earnings of wage and salary workers who usually worked 35 or more hours per week for 50 to 52 weeks during the year. Data prior to 1989 are for civilian workers only.

UNITS: Median money earnings.

Table 8.11 Money Income of Persons 15 Years Old and Older, by Selected Characteristic, 1985

	Hispanic		White		Total	
	male	female	male	female	male	female
Number of persons	6,232	6,366	76,617	82,345	88,474	96,354
persons with incomes:						
under $2,000	444	957	5,180	14,024	6,304	15,848
$2,000-$2,999	199	370	1,808	4,420	2,297	5,425
$3,000-$3,999	264	371	2,190	4,856	2,671	5,958
$4,000-$4,999	203	390	2,095	4,635	2,642	5,693
$5,000-$5,999	368	328	2,169	4,201	2,595	4,848
$6,000-$6,999	301	311	2,278	3,992	2,708	4,648
$7,000-$8,499	416	406	3,402	5,006	4,132	5,855
$8,500-$9,999	325	228	2,896	3,779	3,353	4,288
$10,000-$12,499	599	422	5,895	6,579	6,859	7,576
$12,500-$14,999	392	241	4,527	4,672	5,245	5,339
$15,000-$17,499	431	241	4,940	4,359	5,739	5,012
$17,500-$19,999	281	175	3,869	2,980	4,423	3,432
$20,000-$24,999	468	206	7,521	4,839	8,410	5,513
$25,000-$29,999	349	98	6,374	2,759	7,018	3,194
$30,000-$34,999	221	59	5,324	1,437	5,767	1,633
$35,000-$49,999	267	29	7,730	1,450	8,211	1,585
$50,000-$74,999	71	8	3,421	484	3,588	509
$75,000 and over	224	4	1,603	169	1,669	177
median income	$11,434	$ 6,020	$17,111	$ 7,357	$16,311	$ 7,217
mean income	$14,490	$ 8,178	$21,523	$10,317	$20,652	$10,173

Mean income by:

occupation

managerial, professional specialty	$27,148	$17,471	$34,711	$17,763	$34,201	$17,857
technical, sales, administrative support	17,692	10,461	24,050	10,988	23,293	11,076
service occupations	11,712	5,879	13,161	5,935	12,549	6,104
farming, forestry, fishing	7,451	na	8,241	3,865	8,024	3,762

continued on the next page

Table 8.11 continued

	Hispanic		White		Total	
	male	female	male	female	male	female
Mean income by:						
occupation - continued						
precision production,						
craft, repair	$16,015	$11,217	$20,593	$12,998	$20,277	$12,595
operators, fabricators,						
laborers	13,289	9,649	16,378	9,528	15,971	$9,548
work experience						
worked at full time jobs	$16,297	$11,616	$24,531	$14,556	$23,767	$14,364
worked 50-52 weeks	19,666	14,576	28,140	17,249	27,414	17,028
type of income						
wages and salaries	$14,689	$ 9,557	$21,848	$11,295	$21,056	$11,239
non-farm self-employment	14,026	7,818	16,083	5,885	15,834	5,867
farm self employment	na	na	4,234	1,654	4,184	1,695
property income	877	866	1,866	2,021	1,794	1,937
- interest income	541	605	1,305	1,454	1,254	1,395
transfer payments and all						
other income	4,313	3,686	6,812	4,428	6,572	4,318
- social security or						
railroad retirement	4,793	3,733	5,803	4,330	5,701	4,261
-public assistance and						
supplemental income	3,010	3,696	2,526	2,881	2,560	2,919

SOURCE: U.S. Bureau of the Census, <u>Current Population Reports: Money Income of Households in the United States; March 1985</u>, Series P-60, #156, pp. 107-109, table 31; pp. 135-138, table 35; pp. 141-143, table 37; pp. 160-163, tables 40, 41. C3.186:P-60/156

NOTES: 'Total' includes other races and ethnic groups not shown separately. Number of persons as of March of the <u>following</u> year. Data is based on persons living in households. Persons with incomes under $2,000 includes those with a loss. Occupation represents the longest job held by the person during the year. Educational attainment covers persons 25 years old and older; income covers persons 15 years old and older. 'Property income' includes interest, dividends, net rental income, income from trusts and estates, and net royalty income.

UNITS: Number of persons and persons by income in thousands of persons; median and mean income in dollars.

Table 8.12 Money Income of Persons 15 Years Old and Older, by Selected Characteristic, 1990

	Hispanic		White		Total	
	male	female	male	female	male	female
Number of persons	7,502	7,559	79,555	85,012	92,240	100,680
persons with incomes:						
under $5,000	1,053	2,059	8,539	22,062	10,820	26,337
$5,000-$9,999	1,353	1,502	9,249	16,358	11,312	19,563
$10,000-$14,999	1,298	901	9,529	11,652	11,253	13,566
$15,000-$24,999	1,572	892	16,679	15,162	19,166	17,516
$25,000-$34,999	776	346	12,707	7,547	14,185	8,707
$35,000-$49,999	459	149	10,531	3,895	11,604	4,457
$50,000-$74,999	184	43	5,973	1,382	6,433	1,535
$75,000 and over	72	12	3,274	509	3,446	565
median income	$13,470	$7,532	$21,170	$10,317	$20,293	$10,070
mean income	$17,452	$10,587	$27,142	$14,138	$26,041	$13,913

Mean income by:

work experience

worked at full-time jobs	$19,414	$14,750	$30,498	$19,269	$29,524	$19,010
worked 50-52 weeks	22,859	17,760	34,300	22,198	33,334	21,977

educational attainment

less than 8 years of school	$13,448	$8,269	$15,057	$8,598	$14,914	$8,602
high school graduates	20,400	13,212	25,520	13,955	24,727	13,999
1-3 years of college	25,468	17,852	31,235	17,148	30,340	17,188
4 or more years of college	32,398	20,061	45,709	25,230	44,864	25,388

age

15-24 years old	$9,257	$6,444	$8,915	$7,161	$8,693	$6,998
25-34 years old	17,895	11,262	25,442	15,317	24,365	14,955
35-44 years old	22,419	14,015	35,723	17,724	34,468	17,667
45-54 years old	22,624	13,393	38,632	17,845	37,182	17,831
55-64 years old	21,618	10,117	33,396	14,159	31,899	13,834
65 years old and over	12,280	6,496	20,918	11,864	20,011	11,441

continued on the next page

Table 8.12 continued

	Hispanic		White		Total	
	male	female	male	female	male	female

Mean income by:

marital status

single	$12,286	$10,149	$16,902	$14,504	$16,112	$13,656
married	20,462	10,711	32,362	13,828	31,488	13,858
spouse present	21,316	10,896	32,627	13,805	31,888	13,883
spouse absent	13,428	9,700	25,396	14,255	23,158	13,508
widowed	11,504	9,337	18,528	13,822	17,440	13,190
divorced	22,070	14,471	26,830	19,448	25,787	19,058

SOURCE: U.S. Bureau of the Census, <u>Current Population Reports: Money Income of Households, Families, and Persons in the United States: March 1990</u>, Series P-60, #174, pp. 104-105, table 24; p. 108, table 25; pp. 112-119, table 26; pp. 124-127, table 28; pp. 128-149, table 29; pp. 160-163, table 31. C3.186/2:990

NOTES: 'Total' includes other races and ethnic groups not shown separately. Number of persons as of March of the <u>following</u> year. Data is based on persons living in households. Persons with incomes under $5,000 includes those with a loss. Occupation represents the longest job held by the person during the year. Educational attainment covers persons 25 years old and older; income covers persons 15 years old and older.

UNITS: Number of persons and persons with income, in thousands of persons; percent as a percent as shown; mean and median income in current dollars.

Table 8.13   Money Income of Persons 15 Years Old and Older, by
Selected Characteristic, 2000

	Hispanic		White		Total	
	male	female	male	female	male	female
Total with income	10,253	9,083	82,214	82,901	96,983	99,974
persons with incomes:						
$1-$2,499 or loss	448	980	3,761	8,766	4,718	10,392
$2,500-$4,999	355	803	2,371	5,242	2,998	6,375
$5,000-$7,499	610	1,096	3,341	7,596	4,299	9,389
$7,500-$9,999	595	854	3,248	6,281	3,979	7,490
$10,000-$12,499	903	898	4,378	6,444	5,220	7,755
$12,500-$14,999	685	611	3,406	4,730	4,132	5,726
$15,000-$17,499	958	689	4,023	4,917	4,830	6,015
$17,500-$19,999	615	394	3,334	3,748	4,035	4,505
$20,000-$22,499	825	574	4,432	4,395	5,309	5,445
$22,500-$24,999	416	278	2,933	2,878	3,383	3,446
$25,000-$27,499	562	379	3,930	3,858	4,776	4,806
$27,500-$29,999	304	164	2,219	2,378	2,645	2,808
$30,000-$32,499	536	302	4,238	3,164	5,054	3,882
$32,500-$34,999	186	107	1,842	1,783	2,098	2,133
$35,000-$37,499	356	187	3,394	2,330	4,044	2,832
$37,500-$39,999	162	87	1,789	1,427	2,080	1,707
$40,000-$42,499	317	130	3,152	1,929	3,584	2,367
$42,500-$44,999	110	69	1,393	1,030	1,570	1,202
$45,000-$47,499	191	73	2,209	1,196	2,524	1,411
$47,500-$49,999	85	32	1,352	791	1,545	925
$50,000-$52,499	176	68	2,524	1,306	2,931	1,571
$52,500-$54,999	60	28	961	581	1,087	677
$55,000-$57,499	85	51	1,539	735	1,734	842
$57,500-$59,999	61	21	816	465	917	535

continued on the next page

Table 8.13   continued

	Hispanic		White		Total	
	male	female	male	female	male	female
$60,000-$62,499	134	42	1,974	676	2,221	824
$62,500-$64,999	26	15	727	406	823	438
$65,000-$67,499	59	15	1,084	437	1,217	551
$67,500-$69,999	34	6	563	274	635	333
$70,000-$72,499	54	24	1,037	390	1,223	460
$72,500-$74,999	22	4	491	232	559	263
$75,000-$77,499	57	17	1,058	308	1,152	350
$77,500-$79,999	8	7	425	145	495	182
$80,000-$82,499	33	8	797	233	935	284
$82,500-$84,999	16	6	372	100	411	120
$85,000-$87,499	8	7	502	166	561	179
$87,500-$89,999	13	5	239	92	268	96
$90,000-$92,499	20	6	511	100	584	112
$92,500-$94,999	2	4	189	45	210	58
$95,000-$97,499	4	3	253	91	282	103
$97,500-$99,999	6	0	194	95	242	106
$100,000 and over	157	35	5,210	1,139	5,674	1,278
median income	$19,829	$12,249	$29,696	$16,216	$28,269	$16,188
mean income	$25,863	$16,687	$41,727	$22,564	$40,290	$22,320

SOURCE: U.S. Bureau of the Census and Bureau of Labor Statistics, "Annual Demographic Survey, March Supplement, (Table) PINC-01 Selected Characteristics of People 15 Years and Over, by Total Money Income in 2000, Work Experience in 2000, Race, Hispanic Origin, and Sex,' published 10 December 2001 <http://ferret.bls.census.gov/macro/032001/perinc/new01_000.htm>

NOTES: 'Total' includes other races and ethnic groups not shown separately. Number of persons as of March of the following year.

UNITS: Number of persons with income, in thousands of persons; mean and median income in current dollars.

Table 8.14 Earnings of Persons, by Sex and Type of Hispanic
Origin, 2000

	Mexican	Puerto Rican	Cuban	Central/ South American	Other Hispanic	Total Hispanic
Males	100.0%	100.0%	100.0%	100.0%	100.0%	100.0%
Percent with incomes of:						
$1 to $2,499 or loss	1.0	0.5	0.9	1.2	0.3	1.0
$2,500 to $4,999	0.3	0.3	na	1.1	na	0.4
$5,000 to $9,999	4.3	2.1	2.6	3.8	3.9	4.0
$10,000 to $14,999	17.3	8.6	13.4	14.0	9.1	15.4
$15,000 to $19,999	20.0	13.4	17.1	19.3	10.6	18.7
$20,000 to $24,999	14.4	16.6	9.8	16.0	13.3	14.5
$25,000 to $34,999	19.2	22.3	17.8	17.4	22.5	19.3
$35,000 to $49.999	14.1	18.8	16.6	14.6	21.3	15.0
$50,000 to $74,999	7.4	13.1	10.1	8.6	12.0	8.4
$75,000 and over	2.1	4.3	11.7	4.1	7.0	3.3
Females	100.0%	100.0%	100.0%	100.0%	100.0%	100.0%
percent with incomes of:						
$1 to $2,499 or loss	1.5	0.3	3.3	0.9	1.3	1.3
$2,500 to $4,999	1.5	0.6	na	0.3	1.6	1.1
$5,000 to $9,999	7.1	6.0	5.1	6.3	3.4	6.5
$10,000 to $14,999	24.9	15.6	18.8	22.3	19.2	22.8
$15,000 to $19,999	20.8	18.4	13.1	21.7	17.0	20.0
$20,000 to $24,999	13.6	15.0	11.8	14.2	18.4	14.1
$25,000 to $34,999	15.7	22.7	20.2	14.1	20.0	16.7
$35,000 to $49.999	10.7	13.7	16.3	11.6	11.2	11.5
$50,000 to $74,999	3.5	6.1	8.7	5.0	5.6	4.5
$75,000 and over	0.6	1.5	2.7	3.6	2.4	1.4

SOURCE: U.S. Bureau of the Census, "Current Population Reports: The Hispanic
Population of the United States, 2000, (Tables) 11.2, 11.3. Earnings of
Full-Time, Year-Round Workers 15 Years and Over in 1999 by Sex,
Hispanic Origin and Race: March 2000," published March 6, 2001.
<http: //www..census.gov/population/socdemo/Hispanic/p20-535/tab11-2.txt>
<http: //www..census.gov/population/socdemo/Hispanic/p20-535/tab11-3.txt>

NOTES: 'Other Hispanic origin' includes persons from Spain and persons identifying
themselves generally as Hispanic, Spanish, Spanish-American, Hispano,
Latino, etc. Full-time, year-round workers 15 years old and older.

UNITS: Percent as a percent of total shown (100.0%), mean earnings in current
dollars.

Table 8.15   Per Capita Money Income, 1985 - 1997

	Hispanic	White	Total
1985	$ 9,864	$17,409	$16,427
1986	10,251	18,088	17,090
1987	10,813	18,569	17,507
1988	10,794	18,853	17,804
1989	10,860	19,281	18,193
1990	10,345	18,745	17,667
1991	10,207	18,277	17,225
1992	9,828	18,058	16,985
1993	9,808	18,660	17,524
1994	10,218	19,073	17,929
1995	9,794	19,277	18,143
1996	10,279	19,621	18,552
1997	10,773	20,425	19,241

SOURCE: U.S. Bureau of the Census, Current Population Reports: Measuring 50 Years of Economic Change, Series P-60, #203; p. C-6, table C-3.

NOTES: 'Total' includes other races and ethnic groups not shown separately.

UNITS: Income in 1997 CPI-U adjusted dollars.

Table 8.16 Families Below the Poverty Level, 1980 - 1999

	Hispanic	White	Total
Number below the poverty level			
1980	751	4,195	6,217
1985	1,074	4,983	7,223
1986	1,085	4,811	7,023
1987	1,168	4,567	7,005
1988	1,141	4,471	6,874
1989	1,133	4,409	6,784
1990	1,244	4,622	7,098
1991	1,372	5,022	7,712
1992	1,529	5,255	8,144
1993	1,625	5,452	8,393
1994	1,724	5,312	8,053
1995	1,695	4,994	7,532
1996	1,748	5,059	7,708
1997	1,721	4,990	7,324
1998	1,454	4,829	7,186
1999	1,525	4,377	6,676
Percent below the poverty level			
1980	23.2%	8.0%	10.3%
1985	25.5	9.1	11.4
1986	24.7	8.6	10.9
1987	25.5	8.1	10.7
1988	23.7	7.9	10.4
1989	23.4	7.8	10.3
1990	25.0	8.1	10.7
1991	26.5	8.8	11.5
1992	26.7	9.1	11.9
1993	27.3	9.4	12.3
1994	27.8	9.1	11.6
1995	27.0	8.5	10.8
1996	26.4	8.6	11.0
1997	24.7	8.4	10.3
1998	28.6	8.0	10.0
1999	20.2	7.3	9.3

SOURCE: U.S. Bureau of the Census, Current Population Reports: Poverty in the United States, 1999, Series P-60, #210, pp. B-11 - B-17, table B-3.

NOTES: 'Total' includes other races and ethnic groups not shown separately. Families as of March of the following year.

UNITS: Number below the poverty level in thousands of families; percent as a percent of all families, by race, as shown.

Table 8.17 Families Below the Poverty Level by Type of Family and
Presence of Related Children, 1999

	Hispanic	White	Total
Total Families	7,561	60,256	72,031
Families below poverty level	1,525	4,377	6,676
Married-couple families	728	2,161	2,673
Male householder, no wife present	111	333	472
Female householder, no husband present	686	1,883	3,531
Total families with children under 18 years	5,320	29,841	37,277
Families below poverty level	1,330	3,236	5,129
Married-couple families	607	1,333	1,662
Male householder, no wife present	93	247	350
Female householder, no husband present	630	1,656	3,116

SOURCE: U.S. Bureau of the Census, <u>Current Population Reports: Poverty in the United States</u> 1999, Series P-60, #210, pp. B-11 - B-18, table B-3.

NOTES: Total' includes other races and ethnic groups not shown separately.

UNITS: Number in thousands of families

Table 8.18 Poverty Status of Families, by Type of Hispanic Origin, 2000

	Mexican	Puerto Rican	Cuban	Central/ South American	Other Hispanic	Total Hispanic
Total Families						
Total	4,794	770	385	1,109	504	7,561
Below poverty level	1,018	177	58	181	91	1,525
Married Couple						
Total	3,352	437	296	721	326	5,133
Below poverty level	561	35	31	72	29	728
Male householder, no spouse present						
Total	428	57	18	115	40	658
Below poverty level	68	11	4	22	7	111
Female householder, no spouse present						
Total	1,013	275	70	272	138	1,769
Below poverty level	389	131	24	87	55	686

SOURCE: U.S. Bureau of the Census, "Current Population Reports: The Hispanic Population of the United States, 2000, (Table) 15.1. Poverty Status of Families in 1999 by Family Type, Hispanic Origin and Race of Householder: March 2000;" published March 6, 2001.
<http://www..census.gov/population/socdemo/Hispanic/p20-535/tab15-1.txt>

NOTES: 'Other Hispanic origin' includes persons from Spain and persons identifying themselves generally as Hispanic, Spanish, Spanish-American, Hispano, Latino, etc.

UNITS: Number in thousands of families.

Table 8.19 Persons Below the Poverty Level, 1980 - 2000

	Hispanic	White	Total
Number below the poverty level			
1980	3,491	19,699	29,272
1985	5,236	22,860	33,064
1987	5,422	21,195	32,221
1988	5,357	20,715	31,745
1989	5,430	20,785	31,528
1990	6,006	22,326	33,585
1991	6,339	23,747	35,708
1992	7,592	25,259	38,014
1993	8,126	26,226	39,265
1994	8,416	25,379	38,059
1995	8,574	24,423	36,425
1996	8,697	24,650	36,529
1997	8,308	24,396	35,574
1998	8,070	23,454	34,476
1999	7,439	21,922	32,258
2000	7,155	21,291	31,139
Percent below the poverty level			
1980	25.7%	10.2%	13.0%
1985	29.0	11.4	14.0
1987	28.0	10.4	13.4
1988	26.7	10.1	13.0
1989	26.2	10.0	12.8
1990	28.1	10.7	13.5
1991	28.7	11.3	14.2
1992	29.6	11.9	14.8
1993	30.6	12.2	15.1
1994	30.7	11.7	14.5
1995	30.3	11.2	13.8
1996	29.4	11.2	13.7
1997	27.1	11.0	13.3
1998	25.6	10.5	12.7
1999	22.8	9.8	11.8
2000	21.2	9.4	11.3

SOURCE: U.S. Bureau of the Census, Current Population Reports: Poverty in the United States, 2000, P60-214, pp. 18-21, table A-1 <www.census.gov>

NOTES: 'Total' includes other races and ethnic groups not shown separately.

UNITS: Number below the poverty level in thousands of persons; percent as a percent of all persons, by race, as shown.

Table 8.20   Children Below the Poverty Level, 1980 - 2000

	Hispanic	White	Total
Number below the poverty level			
1980	1,749	7,181	11,543
1985	2,606	8,253	13,010
1990	2,865	8,232	13,431
1991	3,094	8,848	14,341
1992	3,637	8,399	15,294
1993	3,873	9,752	15,727
1994	4,075	9,346	15,289
1995	4,080	8,981	14,665
1996	4,237	9,044	14,623
1997	3,972	8,990	14,113
1998	3,837	8,443	13,467
1999	3,506	7,568	12,109
2000	3,330	7,328	11,633
Percent below the poverty level			
1980	33.2%	13.9%	18.3%
1985	40.3	16.2	20.7
1990	38.4	15.9	20.6
1991	40.4	16.8	21.8
1992	40.0	17.4	22.3
1993	40.9	17.8	22.7
1994	41.5	16.9	21.8
1995	40.0	16.2	20.8
1996	40.3	16.3	20.5
1997	36.8	16.1	19.9
1998	34.4	15.1	18.9
1999	30.3	13.5	16.9
2000	28.0	13.0	16.2

SOURCE: U.S. Bureau of the Census, Current Population Reports: Poverty in the United States, 2000, Series P-60, #214 pp. 23-26, table A-2. <www.census.gov>

NOTES: 'Total' includes other races and ethnic groups not shown separately.

UNITS: Number below the poverty level in thousands of children; percent as a percent of all children under 18 years, by race, as shown.

Table 8.21 Persons 65 Years Old and Over Below the Poverty
Level, 1970 - 1999

	Hispanic	White	Total
Number below the poverty level			
1970	na	4,011	4,793
1979	154	2,911	3,682
1985	219	2,698	3,456
1990	245	2,707	3,658
1991	237	2,802	3,781
1992	269	2,992	3,983
1993	297	2,939	3,755
1994	323	2,846	3,663
1995	342	2,572	3,318
1996	370	2,667	3,428
1997	384	2,569	3,376
1998	356	2,555	3,386
1999	358	2,409	3,167
Percent below the poverty level			
1970	na %	22.6%	24.6%
1979	26.8	13.3	15.2
1985	23.9	11.0	12.6
1990	22.5	10.1	12.2
1991	20.8	10.3	12.4
1992	22.0	10.9	12.9
1993	21.4	10.7	12.2
1994	22.6	10.2	11.7
1995	23.5	9.0	10.5
1996	24.4	9.4	10.8
1997	23.8	9.0	10.5
1998	21.0	8.9	10.5
1999	20.4	8.3	9.7

SOURCE: U.S. Bureau of the Census, Statistical Abstract of the United States, 1994, p. 476, table 731; 2000; p. 476, table 757; 2001; p. 443, table 682 c 3.134:9(year)

NOTES: 'Total' includes other races and ethnic groups not shown separately. Persons as of March of following year.

UNITS: Number below the poverty level in thousands of persons; percent as a percent of all persons, by race, as shown.

Table 8.22   Income of Persons from Specified Sources, 2000

	Hispanic	White	Total
All persons, 15 years and over	19,336	165,115	196,957
Number with income from:			
Earnings	16,077	125,050	149,816
Unemployment compensation	581	3,986	4,967
Workers' compensation	258	1,751	2,104
Social Security	2,201	33,629	38,436
SSI (Supplemental Security Income)	627	3,193	4,685
Public assistance (total)	479	1,416	2,253
Veterans' benefits	81	1,983	2,339
Survivors benefits	112	2,468	2,726
Disability benefits	112	1,229	1,537
Pensions	458	12,937	14,375
Interest	5,058	91,457	102,443
Dividends	1,112	35,887	39,111
Rents, royalties, estates or trusts	530	10,422	11,405
Education	570	6,067	7,578
Child support	478	4,161	5,255
Alimony	16	407	448
Mean income, total from:	$21,552	$32,106	$31,169
Earnings	23,118	34,610	33,688
Unemployment compensation	2,874	2,909	2,917
Workers' compensation	5,014	5,589	5,680
Social Security	7,814	9,343	9,171
SSI (Supplemental Security Income)	4,673	4,710	4,796
Public assistance (total)	3,969	3,206	3,244
Veterans' benefits	8,342	8,829	8,784
Survivors benefits	9,590	11,362	11,147
Disability benefits	6,797	10,373	10,200
Pensions	12,157	13,477	13,422
Interest	869	1,945	1,858
Dividends	1,494	2,676	2,642
Rents, royalties, estates or trusts	2,226	4,556	4,549
Education	3,245	4,620	4,544
Child support	3,755	4,826	4,482
Alimony	8,766	10,054	10,364

SOURCE: U.S. Bureau of the Census and Bureau of Labor Statistics, "Annual Demographic Survey, March Supplement, (Table) PINC-09. Source of Income in 2000--Number With Income and Mean Income of Specified Type in 2000 of People 15 Years Old and Over, by Race, Hispanic Origin and Sex;" published 10 December 2001 <http://ferret.bls.census.gov/macro/032001/perinc/new09_000.htm>

NOTES: 'Total' includes other races and ethnic groups not shown separately. Persons 15 years old and older as of March the following year

UNITS: Number of persons in thousands

Table 8.23   Income of Households from Specified Sources, 1992

	Hispanic	White	Total
All households	6,626	82,083	96,391
one or more members received:			
Social Security	16.8%	28.5%	27.7%
AFDC or other non-SSI cash assistance	12.1	3.7	5.2
SSI	6.9	3.2	4.1
food stamps	18.7	6.6	8.8
housing assistance	7.9	3.3	4.6
free or reduced-price school lunches	21.8	5.5	7.4
employer subsidized health insurance	43.5	54.3	52.9
Medicare	16.5	26.6	25.9
Medicaid	28.5	10.1	12.8
Mean household income from:			
Social Security	$7,306	$8,980	$8,708
AFDC or other non-SSI cash assistance	4,513	3,444	3,489
SSI	4,336	3,651	3,666
food stamps	1,713	1,430	1,564
housing assistance	2,297	1,957	2,022
free or reduced-price school lunches	605	547	553
employer subsidized health insurance	3,231	3,163	3,139
Medicare	3,116	3,652	3,511
Medicaid	1,558	1,696	1,595

SOURCE: U.S. Bureau of the Census, Current Population Reports: Measuring the
Effect of Benefits and Taxes on Income and Poverty: 1992, Series P60-
186RD, pp. 52-54, table 7. C 3.186/P-60/186RD

NOTES: 'Total' includes other races/ethnic groups not shown separately.

UNITS: Number of households in thousands. Percent as a percent of all households,
100.0%. Mean amount of income from specified source per household
receiving that source.

Table 8.24 Child Support Payments Agreed to or Awarded Custodial
Parents, 1997

	Hispanic	White	Total
All Custodial Parents	1,978	10,070	13,987
Child support agreed to or awarded	915	5,998	7,876
Supposed to receive child support	800	5,332	7,006
Received payments	492	3,815	4,720
Full Payments	256	2,356	2,863
Partial Payments	236	1,459	1,857
Did not receive payments	308	1,517	2,286
All Custodial Mothers	1,710	8,264	11,905
Child support agreed to or awarded	798	5,307	7,080
Supposed to receive child support	688	4,752	6,331
Received payments	433	3,475	4,335
Full Payments	234	2,164	2,650
Partial Payments	198	1,311	1,685
Did not receive payments	256	1,277	1,996
All Custodial Fathers	269	1,806	2,082
Child support agreed to or awarded	117	691	796
Supposed to receive child support	112	580	674
Received payments	60	340	385
Full Payments	22	192	213
Partial Payments	37	148	172
Did not receive payments	52	240	289

SOURCE: U.S. Department of Commerce, Current Population Reports, Consumer
Income, Series P60-212, Child Support for Custodial Mothers and
Fathers: 1997, table 4 C3.186:P-60/197

NOTES: 'Total' includes other races/ethnic groups not shown separately.

UNITS: Numbers in thousands. Persons 15 years and older with own children under
21 years of age present from an absent parent as of spring 1998.

Chapter 9: Crime & Corrections

Table 9.01   Victimization Rates for Personal Crimes, 2000

	Hispanic victims	White victims	All Victims
2000			
crimes of violence	28.4	27.1	27.9
rape/sexual assault	0.5*	1.1	1.2
robbery	5.0	2.7	3.2
assault	23.0	23.3	23.5
personal theft	2.4	1.1	1.2

SOURCE: U.S. Department of Justice, Office of Justice Programs, Criminal
Victimization 2000; p. 3, table 1; p. 6, table 2. (data from the *National
Crime Victimization Survey*). <www.ojp.usdoj-gov/pub/cu00.pdf> (10/5/01)

NOTES: 'All victims' includes victims of other races and ethnic groups not shown
separately. Personal crimes include completed and attempted rape,
robbery, assault, and larceny, but exclude homicide.
The National Crime Victimization Survey has been redesigned. Comparisons
of estimates of crime based on previous survey procedures (before
1993) are not recommended.
* Based on 10 or fewer sample cases.

UNITS: Rates per 1,000 persons, 12 years old and over.

Table 9.02 Victimization Rates for Personal Crimes, by Type of Crime, 1999

	Hispanic	White	Total
All personal crimes	35.3	32.7	33.7
Crimes of violence	33.8	31.9	32.8
completed	12.1	9.6	10.1
attempted/threatened	21.7	22.3	22.6
rape/sexual assault	1.9	1.6	1.7
rape/attempted rape	0.4*	0.9	0.9
- rape	0.3*	0.6	0.6
- attempted rape	0.1*	0.3	0.3
sexual assault	1.4	0.7	0.8
robbery	5.6	3.1	3.6
completed/property taken	3.8	2.0	2.4
- with injury	0.5*	0.7	0.8
- without injury	3.2	1.3	1.5
attempted to take property	1.9	1.1	1.2
- with injury	0.7*	0.3	0.3
- without injury	1.1*	0.8	0.9
assault	26.3	27.2	27.4
aggravated	8.9	6.2	6.7
- with injury	2.2	1.9	2.0
- threatened with weapon	6.7	4.2	4.7
simple	17.4	21.1	20.8
- with minor injury	4.4	4.5	4.4
- without injury	13.1	16.6	16.3
purse snatching/pocket picking	1.5	0.8	0.9

SOURCE: U.S. Department of Justice, Bureau of Justice Statistics, <u>Sourcebook of Criminal Justice Statistics 2000</u>; p. 182, table 3.7; p. 183, table 3.8.
J 29.9/2:000

NOTES: 'Total' includes other races and ethnic groups not shown separately. *Based on 10 or fewer sample cases. The National Crime Victimization Survey has been redesigned. Comparisons of estimates of crime based on previous survey procedures (before 1993) are not recommended.
* Based on 10 or fewer sample cases.

UNITS: Rates per 1,000 persons, 12 years old and over.

Table 9.03 Victimization Rates for Property Crimes, by Type of Crime, 2000

	Hispanic households	White households	All households
Property crimes	227.0	173.3	178.1
household burglary	41.7	29.4	31.8
motor vehicle theft	19.7	7.9	8.6
theft	165.6	136.0	137.7

SOURCE: U.S. Department of Justice, Office of Justice Programs, <u>Criminal Victimization 2000</u>; p. 3, table 1; p. 9, table 6. (data from the *National Crime Victimization Survey*). <www.ojp.usdoj-gov/pub/cu00.pdf> (10/5/01)

NOTES: 'Total' includes other races and ethnic groups not shown separately. The National Crime Victimization Survey has been redesigned. Comparisons of estimates of crime based on previous survey procedures (before 1993) are not recommended.

UNITS: Rates per 1,000 households.

Table 9.04   Criminal History Profile of Prisoners Under Sentence of
Death, 2000

	Hispanic	White	Total
U.S. Total	339	1,679	3,593
Prior felony convictions			
Yes	188	962	2,129
No	131	598	1,199
Not reported	na	na	265
Prior homicide convictions			
Yes	23	132	285
No	312	1,521	3,245
Not reported	na	na	63
Legal status at time of capital offense			
Charges pending	12	126	232
Probation	32	140	328
Parole	76	233	572
Prison escapee	3	23	38
Prison inmate	6	39	88
Other status	1	11	21
None	181	953	1,970
Not reported	na	na	344

SOURCE: U.S. Department of Justice, Bureau of Justice Statistics, <u>Capital Punishment</u>
<u>2000</u>, p. 10, table 9. J 29.11:001

NOTES: 'Total' includes other races and ethnic groups not shown separately.

UNITS: Number of jail inmates.

Table 9.05   Prisoners Under Jurisdiction of Federal and State
Correctional Authorities, 1994 - 1997

	Hispanic	White	Total
December 31, 1994			
Total	156,908	464,167	1,054,774
federal institutions	25,226	58,403	95,034
state institutions	131,682	405,764	959,740
December 31, 1995			
Total	174,292	455,021	1,126,287
federal institutions	27,559	60,261	100,250
state institutions	146,733	394,760	1,026,037
December 31, 1996			
Total	186,761	478,308	1,180,524
federal institutions	30,003	61,885	105,544
state institutions	156,758	416,423	1,074,980
December 31, 1997			
Total	198,673	505,513	1,240,962
federal institutions	33,110	65,539	112,973
state institutions	165,563	439,974	1,127,989

SOURCE: U.S. Department of Justice, Bureau of Justice Statistics, Sourcebook
of Criminal Justice Statistics, 1995, pp. 562-563, table 6.26;
1996, pp. 524-525, table 6.26 and table 6.27; 1998, pp. 498-499,
table 6.44 and table 6.45; 1999, pp. 510-511, table 6.34 and
table 6.35. J29.9/6:(YEAR)

NOTES: 'Total' includes other races and ethnic groups not shown separately.
'White' excludes Hispanic persons.

UNITS: Number of prisoners under jurisdictional authority.

Table 9.06   Jail Inmates, 1990 - 2000

	Hispanic	White	Total
1990	14.3%	41.8%	100%
1991	14.2	41.1	100
1992	14.5	40.1	100
1993	15.1	39.3	100
1994	15.4	39.1	100
1995	14.7	40.1	100
1996	15.6	41.6	100
1997	15.7	40.6	100
1998	15.5	41.3	100
1999	15.5	41.3	100
2000	15.1	41.9	100

SOURCE: U.S. Department of Justice, Bureau of Justice Statistics, <u>Prison and Jail Inmates 2000</u>; p. 7, table 9 <www.ojp.usdoj.gov/bjs/pub/pdf/pjimoo.pdf> (accessed: 5 October 2001)

NOTES: 'Total' includes other races and ethnic groups not shown separately. 'White' excludes Hispanic persons.

UNITS: Percent of local jail inmates.

Table 9.07 Prisoners Under Sentence of Death, by State, 2001

	Hispanic	White	Total
United States	330	1,700	3,711
Alabama	1	100	190
Arizona	18	88	125
Arkansas	1	16	40
California	111	236	592
Colorado	2	2	7
Connecticut	1	3	7
Delaware	0	8	18
Florida	36	210	383
Georgia	2	67	132
Idaho	0	20	20
Illinois	10	54	175
Indiana	0	29	42
Kansas	0	4	4
Kentucky	1	33	42
Louisiana	2	27	92
Maryland	0	5	16
Mississippi	0	30	66
Missouri	0	45	79
Montana	0	6	6
Nebraska	1	9	11
Nevada	10	45	92
New Hampshire	0	0	0
New Jersey	0	10	18
New Mexico	1	4	5
New York	1	3	6
North Carolina	3	87	233
Ohio	2	95	202
Oklahoma	4	70	128
Oregon	2	24	29
Pennsylvania	14	73	242
South Carolina	0	39	73
South Dakota	0	5	5
Tennessee	2	60	103
Texas	99	158	450
Utah	2	6	11
Virginia	1	16	28
Washington	0	11	15
Wyoming	0	2	2

SOURCE: U.S. Department of Justice, Bureau of Justice Statistics, Sourcebook of Criminal Justice Statistics, 2000; p. 547, table 6.83. Data from NAACP Legal Defense and Educational Fund. J 29.9/6:000

NOTES: 'Total' includes other races and ethnic groups not shown separately.

UNITS: Number prisoners under sentence of death.

Table 9.08   Chances of Going to State or Federal Prison

	Hispanic	White	Total
For the first time, by age			
20	1.5%	0.4%	1.1%
25	3.6	0.9	2.4
30	5.2	1.4	3.3
35	6.3	1.7	4.0
40	7.5	2.0	4.4
45	8.2	2.1	4.7
50	8.8	2.3	4.9
55	9.1	2.4	5.0
65	9.4	2.5	5.1
Lifetime	9.4	2.5	5.1
At some time during the rest of life, by age			
birth	9.4%	2.5%	5.1%
20	8.7	2.3	4.5
25	6.4	1.7	3.1
30	4.9	1.2	2.1
35	3.8	0.9	1.4
40	2.3	0.6	0.9
45	1.6	0.4	0.6

SOURCE: U.S. Department of Justice, Bureau of Justice Statistics, Lifetime Likelihood
of Going to State or Federal Prison, March 1997, pp. 2-3, tables 1, 2 .
J 29.11/8:997

NOTES: Chances of going to State or Federal Prison for the first time are cumulative
percents. These estimates were obtained by sequentially applying age-
specific first-incarceration rates and mortality rates for each group to a
hypothetical population of 100,000 births. Changes of going to State or
Federal Prison at some time are for persons not previously incarcerated.
These estimates were obtained by subtracting the cumulative percent
first incarcerated for each age from the lifetime likelihood of
incarceration. 'White' and 'Black' exclude persons of Hispanic origin.

UNITS: Percent of all resident population.

Table 9.09 Attitudes Toward the Police, 2000

Question: Do you think the police in your community treat all races fairly or do they tend to
treat one or more of these groups unfairly?

	Hispanic	White	Total
Treat all races fairly	63%	69%	64%
Treat one or more groups unfairly	27	20	26
Don't know	10	10	10

Question: Are you sometimes afraid that the police will stop and arrest you when you are
completely innocent, or not?

	Hispanic	White	Total
Yes, sometimes afraid	22%	14%	17%
No, not afraid	78	86	82

SOURCE: U.S. Department of Justice, Bureau of Justice Statistics, Sourcebook of
Criminal Justice Statistics, 1999; p. 110, tables 2.30, 2.31 J 29.9/6:999

NOTES: Table constructed by SOURCEBOOK staff from data provided by Louis
Harris and Associates, Inc.

UNITS: Percent of persons taking survey who answered with given response.

Table 9.10 Attitudes Toward the Death Penalty, 2001

Question: Do you believe in capital punishment, that is, the death penalty, or are you opposed to
it?

	Hispanic	White	Total
Believe in it	63%	73%	67%
Opposed to it	33	22	26
Not sure/refused	4	6	7

SOURCE: U.S. Department of Justice, Bureau of Justice Statistics, <u>Sourcebook of Criminal
Justice Statistics, 2000; p.</u> 132, table 2.60. 29.9/6:000

NOTES: Table constructed by SOURCEBOOK staff from data provided by Louis Harris and
Associates, Inc.

UNITS: Percent of persons taking survey who answered with given response.

Table 9.11   Inmates Ever Tested for HIV and Results - 1996

	Hispanic	White	Total
Local jails, 1996			
number	45,759	110,023	289,991
percent HIV positive	3.2%	1.4%	2.2%
State prisons, 1997			
number	123,725	257,919	790,128
percent HIV positive	2.5%	1.4%	2.2%
Federal prisons, 1997			
number	18,466	21,128	70,902
percent HIV positive	0.7%	0.3%	0.6%

SOURCE: U.S. Department of Justice, Bureau of Justice Statistics, <u>HIV in Prisons and Jails, 1996</u>; p. 14, table 8. <www.ojp.usobj.gov/bjs/pub/pdf/hivpj96.pdf> accessed October 11, 1999

NOTES: 'Total' includes other races/ethnic groups not shown separately.

UNITS: Percent of inmates tested for HIV (Human Immunodeficiency Virus) and reporting the results.

Table 9.12 Persons Stalked During Their Lifetime, 1996

	Hispanic	White	Total
Male	3.3%	2.1%	2.2%
Female	7.6	8.2	8.1

SOURCE: U.S. Department of Justice, Bureau of Justice Statistics, Sourcebook of Criminal Justice Statistics, 1998; p. 191, table 3.37. J 29.9/2:998

NOTES: 'Total' includes other races/ethnic groups not shown separately. Stalking is defined as a course of Conduct directed at a specific person that involves repeated visual or physical proximity, nonconsensual communication, or verbal, written or implied threats that would cause a reasonable person fear.

UNITS: Rates per 1,000 persons, 12 years old and over.

Chapter 10: Special Topics

Table 10.01   AIDS (Acquired Immunodeficiency Syndrome)
Cases, by Sex and Age, 1985 - 2000

	Hispanic	White	Total
All years*			
children under 13 years old	1,623	1,535	8,401
persons over 13 years old			
male	92,440	295,990	601,471
female	19,359	27,205	119,454
1985			
children under 13 years old	18	26	130
persons over 13 years old			
male	989	4,752	7,508
female	98	142	522
1990			
children under 13 years old	168	158	724
persons over 13 years old			
male	4,752	20,853	36,234
female	730	1,222	4,528
1995			
children under 13 years old	135	117	746
persons over 13 years old			
male	9,146	26,122	56,894
female	2,227	3,050	12,992
1996			
children under 13 years old	123	96	654
persons over 13 years old			
male	8,544	23,096	52,369
female	2,058	2,835	13,115

continued on the next page

Table 10.01 continued

	Hispanic	White	Total
1997			
children under 13 years old	85	62	442
persons over 13 years old			
male	8,219	17,408	45,016
female	2,030	2,458	12,422
1998			
children under 13 years old	70	59	368
persons over 13 years old			
male	6,195	13,868	35,278
female	1,607	2,006	10,442
1999			
children under 13 years old	48	32	255
persons over 13 years old			
male	6,085	12,775	34,254
female	1,608	1,908	10,382
2000 (January-June)			
children under 13 years old	17	18	93
persons over 13 years old			
male	2,674	5,759	15,383
female	763	940	5,074

SOURCE: U.S. Department of Health and Human Services, Health United States, 2001, (Centers for Disease Control and Prevention, National Center for Health Statistics) p. 228, table 53 (data from National Center for HIV, STD, and TB Prevention, Division of HIV/AIDS). HE 20.6223:001

NOTES: 'Total Races' includes other races/ethnic groups not shown separately. 'White' excludes white Hispanics. Data excludes residents of U.S. Territories. Historic data is revised continually on an ongoing basis. Data for all years have been updated through June 30, 1999. * 'all years' includes cases prior to 1985. Data for all years have been updated through June 30, 2000, to include temporarily delayed case reports and may differ from previous editions of Health, United States.

UNITS: Number of cases known to the Centers for Disease Control, by year of report; percent distribution as a percent of total (100.0%).

Table 10.02   Death rates for Human Immunodeficiency Virus (HIV) infection, 1987 - 1999

	Hispanic		White		Total	
	Male	female	male	female	male	female
1987	18.8	2.1	8.7	0.6	10.4	1.1
1990	28.8	3.8	15.7	1.1	18.5	2.2
1992	35.3	5.8	19.0	1.6	23.5	3.2
1993	35.9	6.8	20.0	1.9	25.4	3.9
1994	42.4	8.1	21.2	2.3	27.8	4.9
1995	42.0	9.0	20.7	2.5	27.7	5.3
1996	28.2	6.5	13.2	1.9	19.2	4.3
1997	14.2	3.5	6.0	1.0	9.7	2.7
1998	10.7	2.8	4.6	0.8	7.7	2.3
1999 Preliminary	11.3	3.1	4.9	1.0	8.3	2.6

SOURCE: U.S. Department of Health and Human Services, Health United States, 2001, (Centers for Disease Control and Prevention, National Center for Health Statistics) p. 208, table 43. HE 20.6223:001

NOTES: 'Total' includes other races/ethnic groups not shown separately. Data shown only for states with a Hispanic origin item their death certificates. Age-adjusted rates for all years differ from those shown in previous editions of Health, United States. Age-adjusted rates are calculated using the year 2000 standard population starting with Health, United States, 2001.

UNITS: Number of deaths known to the Centers for Disease Control, by year of report.

Table 10.03   AIDS (Acquired Immunodeficiency Syndrome) Cases,
by Transmission Category, 1985 - 2000

	Hispanic	White	Total
All years*, all transmission categories	111,799	323,195	720,925
men who have sex with men	43,099	220,104	344,619
injecting drug use	36,963	38,896	177,030
men who have sex with men and			
injecting drug use	5,661	24,414	45,991
hemophilia/coagulation disorder	421	3,855	5,057
heterosexual contact	12,496	16,264	72,659
heterosexual contact with			
injecting drug user	4,908	6,326	26,930
transfusion	926	4,975	8,468
undetermined	12,233	14,687	67,101
1990, all transmission categories	5,482	22,075	40,762
men who have sex with men	2,452	16,496	23,687
injecting drug use	2,013	2,053	9,271
men who have sex with men and			
injecting drug use	328	1,637	2,931
hemophilia/coagulation disorder	28	280	349
heterosexual contact	376	647	2,249
heterosexual contact with			
injecting drug user	280	349	1,485
transfusion	82	504	770
undetermined	203	458	1,505
1995, all transmission categories	11,373	29,172	69,886
men who have sex with men	4,176	18,876	30,997
injecting drug use	3,884	4,153	18,820
men who have sex with men and			
injecting drug use	497	2,086	4,093
hemophilia/coagulation disorder	48	327	466
heterosexual contact	1,589	1,930	8,413
heterosexual contact with			
injecting drug user	539	687	2,785
transfusion	74	273	574
undetermined	1,105	1,527	6,523

continued on the next page

Table 10.03   continued

	Hispanic	White	Total
1999			
all transmission categories	7,693	14,683	44,636
men who have sex with men	2,433	8,160	15,444
injecting drug use	1,911	2,144	9,746
men who have sex with men and			
injecting drug use	228	928	1,832
hemophilia/coagulation disorder	13	109	152
heterosexual contact	1,172	1,283	7,034
heterosexual contact with			
injecting drug user	298	388	1,734
transfusion	42	86	259
undetermined	1,894	1,973	10,169
2000, January - June			
all transmission categories	3,437	6,699	20,457
men who have sex with men	979	3,637	6,782
injecting drug use	856	946	4,201
men who have sex with men and			
injecting drug use	108	368	770
hemophilia/coagulation disorder	4	34	44
heterosexual contact	480	510	3,009
heterosexual contact with			
injecting drug user	105	168	720
transfusion	14	51	142
undetermined	996	1,153	5,509

SOURCE: U.S. Department of Health and Human Services, <u>Health United States, 2001</u>, (Centers for Disease Control and Prevention, National Center for Health Statistics) p. 229, table 54 (data from National Center for HIV, STD, and TB Prevention, Division of HIV/AIDS). HE 20.6223:001

NOTES: 'Total' includes other races/ethnic groups not shown separately. 'White' excludes White Hispanics. Data excludes cases of residents of U.S. Territories. 'Hemophilia' includes coagulation disorders. 'Heterosexual' includes persons who have had heterosexual contact with a person with AIDS, or at risk of AIDS, and persons without other identified risks who were born in countries where heterosexual transmission is believed to play a major role although precise means of transmission have not yet been fully determined. * 'All years' includes cases prior to 1985. Data for all years have been updated through June 30, 2000, to include temporarily delayed case reports and may differ from previous editions of Health, United States.

UNITS: Number of cases known to the Centers for Disease Control, by year of report.

Table 10.04   Vaccinations of Children 19-35 Months of Age for Selected
                    Diseases, 1999

	Hispanic	White	Total
1999			
combined series (4:3:1:3)	75%	81%	78%
DTP (4 doses or more)	80	86	83
Polio (3 doses or more)	89	90	90
Measles-containing	90	92	92
Hib (3 doses or more)	92	95	94
Hepatitis B (3 doses or more)	87	89	88
Varicella	61	56	58

SOURCE: U.S. Department of Health and Human Services, Health United States, 2001,
            (Centers for Disease Control and Prevention, National Center for Health
            Statistics) p. 261, table 73 (Data from the National Immunization
            Survey). HE 20.6223:001

NOTES: 'Total' includes other races/ethnic groups not shown separately. 'White'
            excludes White Hispanics. Data excludes cases of residents of U.S.
            Territories.   The 4:3:1:3 combined series consists of 4 doses of
            diphtheria-tetanus-pertussis (DTP) vaccine, 3 doses of polio vaccine, 1
            dose of a measles-containing vaccine, and 3 doses of Haemophilus
            influenza type b (Hib) vaccine. DPT is the Diphtheria-tetanus-pertussis
            vaccine. Hib is the Haemophilus influenza type b (Hib) vaccine.

UNITS: Percent of children 19-35 months of age.

Table 10.05   Health Insurance Coverage, 1990, 1997, 2000

	Hispanic	White	Total
Not covered by private or government health insurance			
total, 1990	28.2%	12.0%	12.9%
total, 1997	34.2%	15.0%	16.1%
total, 2000	43.0%	31.0%	29.5%
children under 18 years	24.9%	10.9%	11.6%

SOURCE: U.S. Bureau of the Census, <u>Current Population Reports: Household Economic Studies - Health Insurance Coverage: 1987-1990</u>, Series P-70, #29; p. 19, table 1 C 3.186/P-70/29 ; <u>Current Population Reports: Consumer Income - Health Insurance Coverage 1997</u>, Series P60-202; p. 2, figure 2; p. 3, figure 5; <u>Current Population Reports: Health Insurance Coverage 2000</u>, Series P60-215; p. 5, figure 2; p. 8, figure 4.

NOTES: 'Total' includes other races and ethnic groups not shown separately.

UNITS: Percent as a percent of all persons in households, 100.0%.

Table 10.06   Selected Characteristics of Farms and Farm Operators, 1997

	Hispanic farms	All farms
Characteristics of farms		
Farms and land in farms		
farms (number)	27,717	47,658
land in farms (acres)	16,406,119	58,738,557
harvested cropland (acres)	2,652,951	3,031,847
Farms by size		
1-9 acres	4,382	8,663
10-49 acres	7,673	14,601
50-139 acres	5,447	11,578
140-219 acres	2,417	4,180
220-499 acres	3,234	4,455
500 acres or more	4,564	4,181
Owned and rented land in farms		
owned land in farms		
farms	24,365	40,869
acres	10,461,612	52,021,859
rented or leased land in farms		
farms	10,238	18,261
acres	5,944,507	6,716,698
1997 Market value of agricultural products sold, (in thousands of dollars)		
total	$3,263,067	$4,231,325
crops (including nursery and greenhouse crops)	2,003,639	2,985,962
livestock, poultry and their products	1,259,428	1,245,363
Farms by value of sales		
less than $1,000	5,082	9,048
$2,500-$9,999	4,113	8,288
$2,500-$9,999	7,151	13,874
$10,000-$19,999	2,739	4,865
$20,000-$24,000	739	1,280
$25,000 or more	7,893	10,303

continued on the next page

Table 10.06   continued

	Hispanic farms	All farms
Farms by North American Industry Classification System		
oilseed and grain farming (1111)	2,547	4,540
vegetable and melon farming (1112)	1,017	2,817
fruit and tree nut farming (1113)	3,859	6,119
greenhouse, nursery, and floriculture production (1114)	1,216	2,397
other crop farming (1119)	3,758	6,048
tobacco farming (11191)	405	1,554
cotton farming (11192)	524	641
sugarcane farming, hay farming, and all other crop farming (11193, 11194, 11199)	2,829	3,853
beef cattle ranching and farming (112111)	11,227	19,434
cattle feedlots (112112)	428	625
dairy cattle and milk production (11212)	637	341
hog and pig farming (1122)	445	1,685
poultry and egg production (1123)	411	738
sheep and goat farming (1124)	622	688
animal aquaculture and other animal production (1125, 1129)	1,550	2,226

Operator characteristics

Residence		
on farm operated	17,526	27,999
not on farm operated	9,406	15,313
not reported	785	4,346
Principal occupation		
farming	13,561	21,584
other	14,156	26,074
Days of work off farm		
none	10,483	16,521
any	16,128	27,789
1-99 days	3,298	4,969
100-199 days	2,856	5,328
200 days or more	9,974	17,492

continued on the next page

Table 10.06 continued

	Hispanic farms	All farms
Characteristics of the farm operator - continued		
Years on present farm		
2 years or less	2,085	3,266
3 or 4 years	2,759	4,282
5 to 9 years	4,933	7,748
10 years or more	14,348	21,330
average on present farm	16.6	16.4
Age		
under 25 years old	235	385
25-34 years old	1,872	2,747
35-44 years old	5,852	8,939
45-54 years old	7,179	12,405
55-59 years old	3,146	5,402
60-64 years old	2,821	5,040
65-69 years old	2,572	4,449
70 years old and over	4,040	8,291
average age	53.6	54.9
Sex		
male	25,184	42,591
female	2,533	5,067

SOURCE: U.S. Bureau of the Census, <u>1997 Census of Agriculture</u>, Vol. 1 Geographic Area Series, Pt. 51, U.S. Summary and State Data, pp. 25-26, table 17. C 3.31/4:992/v. 1/ pt. 51

NOTES: 'All farms' includes farms owned/operated by persons of all races/ethnic groups.

UNITS: Farms, farms by size, farms by organization, farms by value of sales, farms by Standard Industrial Classification, in number of farms; land in farms and harvested crop lands in acres; market value of agricultural products sold in thousands of dollars. Characteristics of farm operators in number of farm operators.

Table 10.07   Summary of Results of the 1999 Consumer Expenditure
Survey

	Hispanic consumer units	White consumer units	All consumer units
Number of consumer units	9,111	95,293	108,465
income before taxes	$33,803	$45,688	$43,951
Average number in consumer unit:			
persons	3.5	2.5	2.5
children under 18 years old	1.3	0.6	0.7
persons 65 and over	0.2	0.3	0.3
earners	1.6	1.4	1.3
vehicles	1.6	2.0	1.9
percent homeowner	44%	68%	65%
Average annual expenditures			
Total	$33,044	$38,323	$36,995
food	5,493	5,149	5,031
food at home	3,556	2,948	2,915
- cereals and bakery products	495	454	448
- meats, poultry, fish, and eggs	1,097	732	749
- dairy products	377	334	322
- fruits and vegetables	663	508	500
- other food at home	924	921	896
food away from home	1,937	2,201	2,116
alcoholic beverages	269	339	318
housing	11,001	12,380	12,057
shelter	6,778	7,225	7,016
- owned dwellings	3,186	4,780	4,525
- rented dwellings	3,420	1,936	2,027
- other lodging	171	509	465
utilities, fuels and public services	2,124	2,374	2,377
household operations	470	695	666
housekeeping supplies	445	516	498
household furnishings and equipment	1,184	1,570	1,499
apparel and services	2,071	1,725	1,743

continued on the next page

Table 10.07   continued

	Hispanic consumer units	White consumer units	All consumer units
transportation	$6,801	$7,275	$7,011
- vehicle purchases	3,362	3,434	3,305
- gasoline and motor oil	1,116	1,096	1,055
- other vehicle expenses	1,979	2,333	2,254
- public transportation	344	412	397
health care	1,119	2,078	1,959
entertainment	1,245	2,022	1,891
personal care products and services	404	409	408
reading	71	170	159
education	366	666	635
tobacco products and smoking supplies	172	313	300
miscellaneous	637	908	867
cash contributions	678	1,269	1,181
personal insurance and pensions	2,718	3,620	3,436
- life and other personal insurance	191	406	394
- pensions and Social Security	2,528	3,214	3,042

SOURCE: U.S. Department of Labor, Bureau of Labor Statistics, <u>Consumer Expenditure Survey, 1999</u>, table 7, accessed 5 November 2001, <ftp://ftp.bls.gov/pub/special.requests/ce/standard/1999/tenracar.txt>

NOTES: 'All consumer units' includes consumer units of all races and ethnic groups.

UNITS: Number of consumer units in thousands; average numbers as shown; average annual expenditures by category, averages in current dollars.

Table 10.08   Occupied Housing Units, by Tenure, 1980 and 1999

	Hispanic householder	White householder	All householders
1980			
All households	4,008	68,810	80,390
owner occupied			
number	1,739	46,671	51,795
percent	43.4%	67.8%	64.4%
renter occupied	2,269	22,139	28,595
1999			
All households	9,041	83,624	102,803
owner occupied			
number	4,087	60,041	68,796
percent	45.2%	71.8%	66.9%
renter occupied	4,955	23,583	34,007

SOURCE: U.S. Bureau of the Census, <u>Statistical Abstract of the United States, 1999</u>, p. 730, table 1214; 2001; p. 606, table 955.   C 3.134(year)

NOTES: 'Total' includes persons of all races/ethnic groups. Persons of Hispanic origin can be of any race.

UNITS: Number of housing units; percent as a percent of total as shown.

Table 10.09   Housing Affordability, Families, 1995

	Hispanic	White	Total
Percent that cannot afford a median priced home in their region using conventional, fixed rate, 30 year financing			
All families	80.8%	47.4%	52.2%
married couples	73.3	39.9	42.2
male householder (no wife present)	87.5	69.2	73.2
female householder (no husband present)	95.7	79.4	84.5
Percent that cannot afford a median priced home in their region using FHA, fixed rate, 30 year financing			
All families	80.3%	46.1%	51.0%
married couples	72.3	38.3	40.6
male householder (no wife present)	87.5	69.6	73.2
female householder (no husband present)	95.9	79.4	84.6

continued on the next page

Table 10.09   continued

	Hispanic	White	Total
Percent that cannot afford a modestly priced home in their region using conventional, fixed rate, 30 year financing			
All families	74.7%	39.6%	44.4%
married couples	65.3	32.2	34.2
male householder (no wife present)	82.5	59.6	64.1
female householder (no husband present)	93.1	72.0	77.7
Percent that cannot afford a modestly priced home in their region using FHA, fixed rate, 30 year financing			
All families	72.6%	37.2%	42.1%
married couples	62.4	29.3	31.4
male householder (no wife present)	82.5	58.2	62.8
female householder (no husband present)	92.6	71.3	77.0

SOURCE: U.S. Bureau of the Census, Current Housing Reports: Who Can Afford to
             Buy A House in 1995?, table 2-2; table 3-2.   C 3.215:H121/99-1

NOTES: 'Total' includes families of all races/ethnic groups.

UNITS: Percent as a percent of families as shown.

Table 10.10   Selected Characteristics of Live Births, 1990 - 1999

	Hispanic births	White births	Total births
1990			
birth weight under 2,500 grams	6.06%	5.70%	6.97%
birth weight under 1,500 grams	1.03	0.95	1.27
mother under 18 years old	6.6	3.6	4.7
mother 18-19 years old	10.2	7.3	8.1
births to unmarried mothers	36.7	20.4	28.0
mother with less than 12 years of school	53.9	22.4	23.8
mother with 16 years or more of school	5.1	19.3	17.5
prenatal care began in 1st trimester	60.2	79.2	75.8
prenatal care began in 3rd trimester or no prenatal care	12.0	4.9	6.1
1999			
birth weight under 2,500 grams	6.38%	6.57%	7.62%
birth weight under 1,500 grams	1.14	1.15	1.45
mother under 18 years old	6.7	3.7	4.4
mother 18-19 years old	10.0	7.2	7.9
births to unmarried mothers	42.2	26.8	33.0
mother with less than 12 years of school	49.1	21.3	21.7
mother with 16 years or more of school	7.4	25.7	24.1
prenatal care began in 1st trimester	74.4	85.1	83.2
prenatal care began in 3rd trimester or no prenatal care	6.3	3.2	3.8

SOURCE: U.S. Department of Health and Human Services, <u>Health United States,</u> <u>2001,</u> (Centers for Disease Control and Prevention, National Center for Health Statistics) p. 135, table 6; p. 138, table 8; p. 139, table 9; p. 140, table 10, p. 142, table 12. HE 20.6223:001

NOTES: Data based on race of the mother. Data on Hispanic-origin available in 48 states plus Washington, DC.

UNITS: Percent, as a percent of all live births, 100.0%.

Table 10.11   Current Users of Cigarettes, Alcohol, Marijuana, and
Cocaine, by Age, 1998

	Hispanic	White	Total
Alcohol			
persons 12-17 years old	19%	21%	19%
persons 18-25 years old	51	65	32
Binge Alcohol			
persons 12-17 years old	6	9	8
persons 18-25 years old	25	38	32
Marijuana			
persons 12-17 years old	8	9	8
persons 18-25 years old	9	15	14
Cocaine			
persons 12-17 years old	1.4	0.9	0.8
persons 18-25 years old	2.7	2.2	2.0

SOURCE: U.S. Department of Health and Human Services, Health United States, 2000, pp. 238-239, table 62   HE 20.6223:000

NOTES: 'Total' includes other races/ethnic groups not shown separately. 'White' excludes Hispanic persons.
Binge Alcohol: Five or more drinks on the same occasion at least once in the past month.

UNITS: Percent as a percent of population by age.

Table 10.12   General Mobility, 1999 to 2000

	Hispanic	White	Total
Total	32,103	221,703	270,219
non-movers	25,347	187,810	226,831
moved to			
same county	4,254	18,811	24,399
different county, same state	1,006	7,135	8,814
different state, same region	335	2,992	4,062
different division, same region	217	1,076	1,261
different region	318	2,633	3,105
abroad	626	1,247	1,746

SOURCE: U.S. Bureau of the Census, Current Population Survey, <u>Geographic Mobility: March 1999 to March 2000</u>, pp. 1-11, table 2.

NOTES: 'Total' includes persons of all races/ethnic groups. Persons of Hispanic origin can be of any race. Mobility data from March 1999 to March 2000.

UNITS: Number of persons one year old and over in thousands.

Table 10.13   Projected Fertility Rates, Women 10-49 Years Old, 2000

	Hispanic women	White women	All women
2000			
Total fertility rate	2,911	2,019	2,055
birth rates			
10-14 years old	2.4	0.8	1.2
15-19 years old	99.4	50.0	56.5
20-24 years old	181.1	108.4	112.5
25-29 years old	151.6	114.8	112.7
30-34 years old	94.3	86.8	85.1
35-39 years old	43.5	35.4	35.5
40-44 years old	10.5	6.8	6.9
45-49 years old	0.6	0.3	0.3

SOURCE: U.S. Bureau of the Census, <u>Statistical Abstract of the United States, 1999</u>, p. 79, table 98; <u>2000</u>; p. 68, table 83; <u>2001</u>; p. 62, table 74. C 3.134(year).

NOTES: 'All women' includes women of other races and ethnic groups not shown separately. The total fertility rate is the number of births that 1,000 women would have in their lifetime if, at each year of age they experienced the birth rates occurring in the specified year. Projections are based on middle fertility assumptions.

UNITS: Total fertility rate and birth rate in births per 1,000 women.

Table 10.14   Selected Characteristics of Persons With a Work
                       Disability, 2000

	Hispanic	White	Total
Persons with a work disability by age			
Total	1,588	12,856	16,744
persons 16-24 years old	133	924	1,347
persons 25-34 years old	243	1,465	2,062
persons 35-44 years old	367	2,932	3,768
persons 45-54 years old	378	3,464	4,516
persons 55-64 years old	468	4,070	5,051
Work disabled as a percent of total population, by age			
Total	7.8%	8.9%	9.5%
persons 16-24 years old	2.6	3.4	3.9
persons 25-34 years old	4.3	4.9	5.5
persons 35-44 years old	7.4	8.0	8.5
persons 45-54 years old	12.5	11.3	12.4
persons 55-64 years old	26.8	20.2	21.6
Percent of work disabled:			
receiving Social Security Income	27.9%	32.6%	31.8%
receiving Food Stamps	24.0	13.9	17.3
covered by Medicaid	43.8	28.6	32.1
residing in public housing	8.4	4.1	6.2
residing in subsidized housing	5.2	3.0	3.7

SOURCE: U.S. Bureau of the Census, Statistical Abstract of the United States, 2001,
           p. 351, table 538 (data from the Current Population Survey). C 3.134:001

NOTES: 'Total' includes other races and ethnic groups not shown separately. Covers
           the civilian noninstitutional population and members of the armed forces
           living off post or with members of their families on post. Persons are
           classified as having a work disability if they (1) have a health problem or
           disability which prevents them from or which limits the kind or amount
           of work they can do; (2) have a service disability or ever retired or left a
           job for health reasons; (3) did not work in survey reference week or
           previous year because of long-term illness or disability; or, (4) are under
           age 65 and are covered by Medicare or receive Supplemental Security
           Income.

UNITS: Persons with a work disability in thousands of persons; work disabled as a
           percent of total population in percent; percent of the work disabled by
           characteristic as a percent of the work disabled.

Table 10.15   Percentage of Adults Engaging in Leisure-Time Physical
Activity, 1997, 1998

	Hispanic	White	Total
1997			
no participation in physical activity	36.6%	27.6%	29.5%
participates in regular, sustained activity	17.1	20.3	19.6
participates in regular, vigorous activity	8.6	14.0	12.9
1998			
no participation in physical activity	38.4%	26.7%	28.7%
participates in regular, sustained activity	17.4	21.6	20.8
participates in regular, vigorous activity	11.4	14.0	13.6

SOURCE: U.S. Bureau of the Census, Statistical Abstract of the United States, 1999,
p. 157, table 248; 2000; p. 145, table 232 (data from National Center for
Chronic Disease Prevention and Health Promotion), C 3.134:999

NOTES: 'Total' includes other races and ethnic groups not shown separately.
'Regular, sustained activity' is any type or intensity of activity that occurs
5 or more times per week and 30 minutes or more per occasion. 'Regular,
vigorous activity' is rhythmic contraction of large muscle groups
performed 3 times per week or more for at least 20 minutes per occasion.

UNITS: Percent of persons 18 years of age and over.

Table 10.16   Health Care Coverage for Persons Under 65 Years of Age, by Type of Coverage, 1984 - 1998

	Hispanic	White	Total
1984			
Private insurance	56.3%	79.7%	76.6%
Private insurance obtained through workplace	52.3	71.9	68.9
Medicaid or other public assistance	13.1	5.0	7.3
not covered	29.0	13.3	14.2
1993			
private insurance	48.3%	75.1%	71.3%
private insurance obtained through workplace	44.0	68.8	65.3
Medicaid or public assistance	18.7	8.1	11.1
not covered	32.6	15.6	16.5
1998			
private insurance	49.9%	75.9%	72.3%
private insurance obtained through workplace	46.3	69.2	66.1
Medicaid or other public assistance	14.1	6.7	8.8
not covered	34.0	15.2	16.5

SOURCE: U.S. Department of Health and Human Services, Health United States, 1999, pp. 299-300, table 129; 2001, (Centers for Disease Control and Prevention, National Center for Health Statistics) pp. 348-349, table 128; pp. 351-352, table 129; pp. 353-354, table 130 (data from the National Health Interview Survey). HE 20.6223(year)

NOTES: 'Total' includes other races not shown separately. Medicaid includes persons receiving AFDC (Aid to Families with Dependent Children) or SSI (Supplemental Security Income), or those with a current Medicaid card. Not covered includes those persons not covered by private insurance, Medicaid, Medicare, and military plans. Data **are** age-adjusted. The questionnaire changed in 1997 compared with previous years.

UNITS: Percent of the population.

Table 10.17   Health Care Coverage for Persons 65 Years of Age
and Over, by Type of Coverage, 1984 - 1998

	Hispanic	White	Total
1984			
Private insurance	40.5%	76.8%	73.5%
Private insurance obtained through workplace	25.4	40.9	39.1
Medicaid or other public assistance	24.9	5.0	6.9
Medicare only	28.5	16.5	17.7
1993			
Private insurance	39.8%	80.9	77.3%
Private insurance obtained through workplace	18.8	42.7	40.9
Medicaid or other public assistance	31.1	5.6	7.4
Medicare only	26.5	12.4	14.0
1998			
Private insurance	29.1%	70.3%	66.7%
Private insurance obtained through workplace	17.8	37.9	36.5
Medicaid or other public assistance	27.2	6.4	8.1
Medicare only	38.4	21.8	23.3

SOURCE: U.S. Department of Health and Human Services, Health United States, 1999,
pp. 301-302, table 130; 2001, (Centers for Disease Control and
Prevention, National Center for Health Statistics) pp. 355-356, table 131
(data from the National Health Interview Survey). HE 20.6223(year)

NOTES: 'Total' includes other races/ethnic groups not shown separately. Medicaid
includes persons receiving AFDC (Aid to Families with Dependent
Children) or SSI (Supplemental Security Income), or those with a current
Medicaid card. Not covered includes those persons not covered by
private insurance, Medicaid, Medicare, and military plans. Data **are**
age-adjusted.
The questionnaire changed in 1997 compared with previous years.

UNITS: Percent of the population.

Table 10.18   Births and Birth Rates, by Age of the Mother, preliminary
2000

	Hispanic	White	Total
Live births	815,778	3,202,932	4,064,948
Fertility rate	105.9	66.7	67.6
Birth rate per 1,000 women, by age group			
10-14 years old	1.9	0.6	0.9
15-19 years old	94.4	43.9	48.7
20-24 years old	184.6	108.3	112.5
25-29 years old	170.8	124.9	121.7
30-34 years old	109.0	97.6	94.2
35-39 years old	48.6	40.7	40.3
40-44 years old	11.6	7.7	7.9
45-49 years old	0.6	0.4	0.5

SOURCE: U.S. Department of Health and Human Services National Vital Statistics Report: Births: Preliminary Data for 2000, Volume 49, No. 5, July 24, 2001; p. 9, table 2; p. 10, table 3.   HE 20.6217:001

NOTES: 'Total' includes other races and ethnic groups not shown separately. Data based on race of the mother. Fertility rate is the total number of births, regardless of age of mother, per 1,000 women aged 15-44 years.

UNITS: Live births in number of births; rates as shown.

Table 10.19 Birth Rates for Women 15-44 Years of Age, by Live Birth Order, preliminary 2000

	Hispanic mothers	White mothers	All mothers
All live births	105.9	66.7	67.6
first child	39.5	26.9	27.1
second child	32.3	22.0	22.0
third child	19.9	11.2	11.3
fourth child and over	14.2	6.6	7.2

SOURCE: U.S. Department of Health and Human Services National Vital Statistics Report: Births: Preliminary Data for 2000, Volume 49, No. 5, July 24, 2001; p. 10, table 3. HE 20.6217:001

NOTES: 'All mothers' includes mothers of other races and ethnic groups not shown separately. Data based on race of the mother.

UNITS: Live births per 1,000 women 15-44 years of age.

Table 10.20   Death Rates for Malignant Neoplasms of the Breast, for Females, by Age, 1985 and 1999

	Hispanic women	White women	All Women
1985			
All ages, age adjusted rate	16.3	33.1	33.0
All ages, crude rate	8.8	34.7	32.8
35-44 years old	10.4	16.8	17.5
45-54 years old	26.4	46.8	47.1
55-64 years old	43.5	84.7	84.2
65-74 years old	40.9	109.9	107.8
75-84 years old	64.5	138.8	136.2
85 years old and over	85.7	180.9	178.5
1999, preliminary			
All ages, age adjusted rate	15.4	26.4	27.0
All ages, crude rate	9.9	30.7	29.5
35-44 years old	8.5	10.8	12.1
45-54 years old	24.1	31.4	33.5
55-64 years old	35.3	58.1	59.9
65-74 years old	46.3	89.9	89.9
75-84 years old	63.4	131.7	131.3
85 years old and over	97.9	204.9	202.6

SOURCE: U.S. Department of Health and Human Services, Health United States, 2001, (Centers for Disease Control and Prevention, National Center for Health Statistics) p. 202, table 41. HE 20.6223:001

NOTES: 'All Women' includes women of other races/ethnic groups not shown separately. Data excludes deaths of nonresidents of the United States. *Indicates data based on fewer than 20 deaths. Age-adjusted rates for all years differ from those shown in previous editions of Health, United States. Age-adjusted rates are calculated using the year 2000 standard population starting with Health, United States, 2001.

UNITS: Rate is the number of deaths per 100,000 resident female population, by age group.

Table 10.21   Death Rates for Motor Vehicle Accidents, by Sex
and Age, 1999

	Hispanic		White		Total	
	male	female	male	female	male	female
1999 (preliminary)						
All ages, age adjusted	22.0	8.1	21.8	9.9	21.8	9.8
All ages, crude	21.2	7.6	21.6	10.2	21.4	9.9
under 1 year	na	na	5.0	3.8	4.9	4.7
1-14 years old	4.9	3.8	4.9	3.6	5.1	3.7
15-24 years old	38.0	11.7	38.6	17.4	36.9	16.3
25-34 years old	30.8	8.1	26.5	9.5	26.5	9.3
35-44 years old	21.9	6.7	21.0	8.8	21.3	8.9
45-64 years old	20.0	8.5	19.1	8.6	19.8	8.8
65 years old and over	27.3	12.9	31.3	16.7	31.2	16.4

SOURCE: U.S. Department of Health and Human Services, Health United States, 2001,
(Centers for Disease Control and Prevention, National Center for Health
Statistics) pp. 210-212, table 45. HE 20.6223:001

NOTES: 'Total' includes other races and ethnic groups not shown separately.
Excludes deaths of nonresidents of the United States. *Indicates data
based on fewer than 20 deaths. Age-adjusted rates for all years differ
from those shown in previous editions of Health, United States. Age-
adjusted rates are calculated using the year 2000 standard population
starting with Health, United States, 2001.

UNITS: Rate is the number of deaths per 100,000 resident population.

Table 10.22   Death Rates for Assault (Homicide), by Sex and Age, 1999

	Hispanic		White		Total	
	male	female	male	female	male	female
1999, Preliminary						
All ages, age adjusted	13.8	2.8	5.5	2.1	9.3	2.9
All ages, crude	15.2	3.0	5.6	2.1	9.6	2.9
under 1 year	7.1	7.6	7.5	5.3	9.3	7.6
1-14 years old	1.9	1.3	1.1	1.0	1.6	1.3
15-24 years old	34.9	4.9	10.5	3.0	21.7	4.4
25-44 years old	20.6	3.7	7.9	3.0	13.7	4.3
45-64 years old	9.3	2.5	4.4	1.6	6.2	2.0
65 years old and over	4.6	*	2.8	1.6	3.5	1.8

SOURCE: U.S. Department of Health and Human Services, <u>Health United States, 2001</u>, (Centers for Disease Control and Prevention, National Center for Health Statistics) pp. 214-216, table 46. HE 20.6223:001

NOTES: 'Total' includes other races/ethnic groups not shown separately. Excludes deaths of nonresidents of the United States. *Based on fewer than 20 deaths. Age-adjusted rates for all years differ from those shown in previous editions of Health, United States. Age-adjusted rates are calculated using the year 2000 standard population starting with Health, United States, 2001.

UNITS: Rate is the number of deaths per 100,000 resident population

Table 10.23   Death Rates for Suicide, by Sex and Age, 1999

	Hispanic		White		Total	
	male	female	male	female	male	female
1999 (preliminary)						
All ages, age adjusted	10.7	1.9	19.3	4.4	18.1	4.0
All ages, crude	9.1	1.7	19.1	4.5	17.5	4.1
15-24 years old	11.9	2.0	17.8	3.2	17.1	3.1
25-44 years old	13.1	2.5	23.8	6.2	22.3	5.6
45-64 years old	11.9	2.5	22.9	6.7	21.2	6.0
65 years old and over	17.4	2.2	34.5	4.6	32.1	4.3

SOURCE: U.S. Department of Health and Human Services, Health United States, 2001, (Centers for Disease Control and Prevention, National Center for Health Statistics) pp. 217-219, table 47. HE 20.6223:001

NOTES: 'Total' includes other races and ethnic groups not shown separately. Excludes deaths of nonresidents of the United States. *Indicates data based on fewer than 20 deaths. Age-adjusted rates for all years differ from those shown in previous editions of Health, United States. Age-adjusted rates are calculated using the year 2000 standard population starting with Health, United States, 2001.

UNITS: Rate is the number of deaths per 100,000 resident population.

Table 10.24   Dental Visits in the Past Year by Poverty Status, 1999

	Hispanic	White	Total
1999			
Poor			
2-17 years old	49.6%	62.9%	57.8%
18-64 years old	39.7	50.6	46.0
65 years old and over	32.1	32.2	31.9
Non-Poor			
2-17 years old	72.0%	81.8%	79.9%
18-64 years old	62.0	72.4	70.8
65 years old and over	58.9	65.4	64.4

SOURCE: U.S. Department of Health and Human Services, <u>Health United States, 2001</u>, (Centers for Disease Control and Prevention, National Center for Health Statistics) p. 276, table 80 (data from the National Health Interview Survey). HE 20.6223:01

NOTES: 'Total' includes other races and ethnic groups not shown separately. 'White' excludes white Hispanics. Data excludes residents of U.S. Territories. Poor persons are defined as below the poverty threshold. Non-poor persons have incomes of 200 percent or greater than the poverty threshold.

UNITS: Percent of persons with a dental visit in the past year.

Table 10.25   Hispanic Owned Firms, by Major Industry Group, 1992, 1997

| | all firms | | firms with paid employees | | | |
	firms	sales & receipts	firms	sales & receipts	employees	annual payroll
1992						
All industries	771,708	$72,824,270	115,364	$57,187,370	691,056	$10,768,112
agricultural services, forestry and fishing	31,600	1,464,572	3,985	935,079	19,174	233,781
mining	1,327	304,926	194	250,485	1,527	33,555
construction	97,476	8,212,208	20,192	6,447,317	76,882	1,417,290
manufacturing	18,461	6,157,555	5,209	5,827,194	65,920	1,280,030
transportation and public utilities	47,797	3,702,744	5,100	2,373,189	35,484	606,617
wholesale trade	17,727	12,489,034	5,434	11,687,451	37,547	859,658
retail trade	107,846	17,730,517	27,641	15,116,613	197,626	2,001,152
finance, insurance, and real estate	49,231	4,831,923	5,087	2,774,196	23,177	472,149
services	347,297	16,787,257	40,863	11,558,361	231,977	3,836,093
industries not classified	52,945	1,143,533	1,660	217,485	1,743	27,787
1997						
All industries	1,199,896	$186,274,582	211,884	$158,674,537	1,388,746	$29,830,028
agricultural services, forestry and fishing	40,040	2,279,397	5,925	1,309,733	25,955	416,702
mining	1,909	429,446	325	367,442	3,569	97,854
construction	152,573	21,923,384	31,478	19,146,212	168,873	4,218,419
manufacturing	25,552	28,684,759	10,173	27,719,404	171,738	4,549,598
transportation and public utilities	84,554	8,293,935	12,735	5,605,332	79,682	1,587,106
wholesale trade	31,480	40,386,625	14,125	38,746,137	94,281	2,388,988
retail trade	155,061	32,280,310	48,713	28,599,447	324,474	3,892,182
finance, insurance and real estate	56,629	6,644,826	9,944	4,728,312	34,783	949,006
services	500,449	39,177,767	70,838	30,406,573	463,889	11,297,362
industries not classified	151,931	6,174,133	7,909	2,045,945	21,502	432,812

SOURCE: U.S. Bureau of the Census, 1992 Economic Censuses MB92-2 Survey of Minority-Owned Business Enterprises: Hispanic, pp. 13-14, table 1. C 3.258:92-2
1997 Economic Censuses Survey of Minority-Owned Business Enterprises: Hispanic, pp. 17-18, table 1. EC97CS-4

NOTES: Data from the 1992 and 1997 Economic Censuses.

UNITS: Firms in number of firms; sales and receipts in thousands of dollars; employees in number of employees; annual payroll in thousands of dollars.

Table 10.26   Abortions, 1992 - 1998

	Hispanic	White	Total
1992	30.7	23.6	33.5
1993	28.9	23.1	33.4
1994	27.8	21.7	32.1
1995	26.5	20.4	31.1
1996	27.6	20.2	31.4
1997	26.8	19.4	30.6
1998*	28.9	18.8	26.2

SOURCE: U.S. Department of Health and Human Services, <u>Health, United States, 2001,</u> (Centers for Disease Control and Prevention, National Center for Health Statistics) p. 148, table 16. HE 20.6223:001

NOTES: 'Total' includes women of other races/ethnic groups not shown separately. "White" includes women of Hispanic ethnicity. *1998 data preliminary. CA, AK, NH, OK did not report abortion data in 1998.

UNITS: Abortions per 100 live births.

Glossary

ACUTE CONDITION see **CONDITION (HEALTH)**.

AGE ADJUSTMENT
Age adjustment, using the direct method, is the application of the age specific rates in a population of interest to a standardized age distribution in order to eliminate the differences in observed rates that result from age differences in population composition. This adjustment is usually done when comparing two or more populations at one point in time, or one population at two or more points in time.

AGGRAVATED ASSAULT see **CRIME**.

ARSON see **CRIME**.

AVERAGE see **MEAN; MEDIAN**.

BED (HOSPITAL; NURSING HOME)
Any bed that is staffed for use by inpatients is counted as a bed in a facility.

BED-DISABILITY DAY see **DISABILITY DAY**.

BIRTH see **LIVE BIRTH**.

BURGLARY see **CRIME**.

CAUSE OF DEATH
For the purpose of national mortality statistics, every death is attributed to one underlying condition, based on information reported on the death certificate and utilizing the international rules (International Classifications of Disease) for selecting the underlying cause of death from reported conditions. Selected causes of death are shown on tables.

CHRONIC CONDITION see **CONDITION (HEALTH)**.

CIVILIAN LABOR FORCE
All persons (excluding members of the Armed Forces) who are either employed or unemployed. (The experienced civilian labor force is a subgroup of the civilian labor force, composed of all persons, employed and unemployed, that have worked before.)
Employed persons are those persons 16 years old and over who were either a) "at work"- those who did any work at all as paid employees, or in their own business or profession, or on their own farm, or worked 15 or more hours as unpaid workers on a family farm or in a family business; or b) "with a job but not at work"- those who did not work during the reference period but had jobs or businesses from which they were temporarily absent due to illness, bad weather, industrial dispute, vacation, or other personal reasons. Excluded from the employed are persons whose only activity consisted

of work around the house or volunteer work for religious, charitable, and similar organizations.

Employed persons are classified as either **full-time workers**, those who worked 35 hours or more per week; or **part-time workers**, those who worked less than 35 hours per week.

Unemployed persons are those who were neither "at work" nor "with a job, but not at work" <u>and</u> who were a) looking for work, and b) available to accept a job. Also included as unemployed are persons who are waiting to be called back to a job from which they have been laid off. The unemployed are divided into four groups according to reason for unemployment:

--**job losers** (including those who have been laid off)

--**job leavers** who have left their job voluntarily

--**reentrants**, persons who have worked before and are reentering the labor force

--**new entrants** to the labor force looking for work

CIVILIAN NONINSTITUTIONAL POPULATION see **POPULATION.**

CIVILIAN POPULATION see **POPULATION.**

COLLEGE

A postsecondary school which offers a general or liberal arts education, usually leading to an associate, bachelor's, master's, doctor's, or first professional degree. Junior colleges and community colleges are included. See also **Institution of Higher Education; University.**

COMMUNITY HOSPITAL

All non-federal short term hospitals, excluding hospital units of institutions, whose services are available to the public. **Short term hospitals** are those where the average length of stay is less than 30 days.

CONDITION (HEALTH)

A health condition is a departure from a state of physical or mental well-being. Based on duration, there are two categories of conditions: acute and chronic.

An **acute condition** is one that has lasted less than three months, and has involved either a physician visit (medical attention) or restricted activity.

A **chronic condition** is any condition lasting three months or more, or is one classified as chronic regardless of the time of onset. See also **Health Limitation of Activity.**

CONSOLIDATED METROPOLITAN STATISTICAL AREA (CMSA)

A geographic area concept introduced in June, 1984, which, in combination with Metropolitan Statistical Area (MSA), and Primary Metropolitan Statistical Area (PMSA), replace the Standard Metropolitan Statistical Area (SMSA) concept. CMSAs are designated in accordance with criteria established by the federal Office of Management and Budget (OMB). In general CMSAs are MSAs with a population of one million or more, and which have component PMSAs. See also **Metropolitan Statistical Area.**

CONSUMER EXPENDITURE SURVEY

A survey of current consumer expenditures reflecting the buying habits of American consumers. Begun in 1979 and conducted jointly by the U.S. Bureau of Labor Statistics and the U.S. Bureau of the Census, the survey consists of two parts: an interview panel survey in which the expenditures of consumer units are obtained in five interviews conducted every three months, and a diary or record keeping survey completed by the participating households for two consecutive one-week periods. See also **Consumer Unit.**

The Consumer Expenditure Survey, which collects data on expenditures, should not be confused with the Consumer Price Index, which measures the average change in prices of consumer goods and services.

CONSUMER UNIT

An entity used as the basis of the Consumer Expenditure Survey. A consumer unit comprises either

--all the members of a particular household who are related by blood, marriage, adoption, or other legal arrangements; or

--a person living alone or sharing a household with others, or living as a roomer in a private home or lodging house or in a permanent living quarters in a hotel or motel, but who is financially independent; or

--two or more persons living together who pool their income to make joint expenditure decisions.

A consumer unit may or may not be a household.

CRIME

A crime is an action which is prohibited by law. Their are two major statistical programs which measure crime in the United States. The first is the Uniform Crime Reporting (UCR) program, administered by the FBI. The Bureau receives monthly and annual reports from most police agencies around the country (covering approximately 97% of the population). These reports contain information on eight major types of crime (called collectively, serious crime), which are known to police. Serious crime consists of four violent crimes (murder and non-negligent manslaughter, which includes willful felonious homicides and is based on police investigations rather than determinations of a medical examiner; forcible rape, which includes attempted rape; robbery, which includes stealing or taking anything of value by force or violence, or by threat of force or violence, and includes attempted robbery; and aggravated assault which includes intent to kill), and four property crimes (burglary, which includes any unlawful entry to commit a felony or theft and includes attempted burglary and burglary followed by larceny; larceny, which includes theft of property or articles of value without use of force, violence, or fraud, and excludes embezzlement, con games, forgery, etc.; motor vehicle theft, which includes all cases where vehicles are driven away and abandoned, but excludes vehicles taken for temporary use and returned by the taker; and arson, which includes any willful or malicious burning or attempt to burn, with or without the intent to defraud, of a dwelling house, public building, motor vehicle, aircraft, or personal property of another.)

The second approach to the measurement of crime is through the National Crime Survey (NCS) administered by the Bureau of Justice Statistics. The survey is based on a representative sample of approximately 49,000 households, inhabited by about 102,000 persons age 12 and over. Although the categories of crime are similar to those used by the FBI in the UCR, the NCS is based on reports of victimization directly by victims, as opposed to crimes reported to police as in the UCR. As might be imagined, not all crimes are reported or known to police, therefore NCS estimates of crime tend to be significantly higher than UCR figures. The NCS also differs from the UCR in that only crimes whose victims can be interviewed are included (hence there are no homicide statistics), and only victims who are 12 years old or older are counted. The two central concepts in the NCS are victimization, which is the specific criminal act as it affects a single victim, and a criminal incident, which is a specific criminal act involving one or more victims. Thus in regard to personal crime, there are more victimizations, than incidents.

DEATH see **CAUSE OF DEATH; INFANT MORTALITY.**

DISABILITY

The presence of a physical, mental, or other health condition which has lasted six or more months and which limits or prevents a particular type of activity. See also **Work Disability.**

DISABILITY DAY

A day on which a person's usual activity is reduced because of illness or injury. There are four types of disability days (which are not mutually exclusive). They are

--a **restricted-activity day**, a day on which a person cuts down on his or her usual activities because of illness or an injury.

--a **bed-disability day,** a day on which a person stays in bed more than half of the daylight hours (or normal waking hours) because of a specific illness or injury. All hospital days are bed-disability days. Bed disability days may also be work-loss days or school loss days.

--a **work-loss day**, a day on which a person did not work at his or her job or business for at least half of his or her normal workday because of a specific illness or injury. Work loss days are determined only for employed persons.

--a **school-loss day**, a day on which a child did not attend school for at least half of his or her normal schoolday because of a specific illness or injury. School-loss days are determined only for children 6 to 16 years of age.

DISPOSABLE INCOME see **INCOME.**

EMPLOYED PERSONS see **CIVILIAN LABOR FORCE.**

EMPLOYMENT STATUS see **LABOR FORCE STATUS.**

ENROLLMENT
The total number of students registered in a given school unit at a given time, generally in the fall of the year. See also **Full-Time Enrollment; Part-Time Enrollment.**

EVER MARRIED PERSONS see **MARITAL STATUS.**

EXPERIENCED CIVILIAN LABOR FORCE
That portion of the Civilian Labor Force, both employed and unemployed, that have worked before. Excludes new entrants to the Civilian Labor Force. See also **Civilian Labor Force.**

EXPERIENCED WORKER see **EXPERIENCED CIVILIAN LABOR FORCE.**

FAMILY
A type (subgroup) of household in which there are two or more persons living together (including the householder) who are related by birth, marriage, or adoption. All such related persons in one housing unit are considered as members of one family. (For example, if the son or daughter of the family householder and that son's or daughter's spouse and/or children are members of the household, they are all counted as part of the householder's family.) However, non-family members who are not related to the householder (such as a roomer or boarder and his or her spouse, or a resident employee and his or her spouse who are living in), are not counted as family members but as unrelated individuals living in a family household. Thus for Census purposes, a housing unit can contain only one household, and a household can contain only one family. See also **Family Type; Household; Householder; Unrelated Individual.**

FAMILY INCOME see **INCOME.**

FAMILY TYPE
Families are classified by type according to the sex of the householder and the presence of a spouse and children. The three main types of households are: **Married Couples,** in which a husband and wife live together (with or without other persons in the household); **Male Householder, No Wife Present,** in which a male householder lives together with other members of his family but without a wife; and **Female Householder, No Husband Present,** in which a female householder lives together with other members of her family but without a husband. See also **Family; Family Household; Household.**

FARM
As defined by the Bureau of the Census (and adopted by the Department of Agriculture), a farm is any place from which $1,000 or more of agricultural products were sold, or would have been sold during a given year. Control of the farm may be exercised through ownership or management, or through a lease, rental or cropping

arrangement. In the case of landowners who have one or more tenants or renters, the land operated by each is counted as a separate farm. This definition has been in effect since 1974.

FARMLAND

All land under the control of a farm operator, including land not actually under cultivation or not used for pasture or grazing. Rent free land is included as part of a farm only if the operator has sole use of it. Land used for pasture or grazing on a per head basis that is neither owned nor leased by the farm operator is not included except for grazing lands controlled by grazing associations leased on a per acre basis.

FARM INCOME

Gross farm income comprises cash receipts from farm marketings of crops and livestock, federal government payments made directly to farmers for farm-related activities, rental value of farm homes, value of farm products consumed in farm homes, and other farm-related income such as machine hire and custom work.

FULL-TIME ENROLLMENT (HIGHER EDUCATION)

The number of students enrolled in higher education courses with a total credit load equal to at least 75% of the normal full-time course load.

FULL-TIME WORKERS see CIVILIAN LABOR FORCE.

HEALTH LIMITATION OF ACTIVITY

A characteristic of persons with chronic conditions. Each person identified as having a chronic condition is classified as to the extent to which his or her activities are limited by the condition as follows:

--persons unable to carry on a major activity (that is the principal activity of a person of his or her age-sex group: for persons 1-5 years of age, it refers to ordinary play with other children; for persons 6-16 years of age, it refers to school attendance; for persons 17 years of age and over, it usually refers to a job, housework, or school attendance.)

--persons limited in the amount or kind of major activity performed.

--persons not limited in major activity, but otherwise limited.

--persons not limited in activity.

See also **Condition (Health).**

HEALTH MAINTENANCE ORGANIZATION (HMO)

A prepaid health plan delivering comprehensive care to members through designated providers, having a fixed monthly payment for health care services, and requiring members to be in the plan for a specified period of time (usually one year). HMOs are distinguished by the relationship of the providers to the plan. HMO model types are: **Group** -- an HMO that delivers health services through a physician group controlled by the HMO, or an HMO that contracts with one or more independent group practices to provide health services; **Individual Practice Association (IPA)** -- an HMO that contracts directly with physicians in independent practice, and/or contracts with one or more associations of physicians in independent practice, and/or contracts with one or more multi-specialty group practices (but the plan is predominantly organized around solo-single specialty practices).

HIGHER EDUCATION see **INSTITUTION OF HIGHER EDUCATION.**

HISPANIC ORIGIN

An aspect of a person's ancestry. The Bureau of the Census in many of its survey asks persons if they are of Hispanic origin. There are four main subcategories of Hispanic origin: Mexican, Puerto Rican, Cuban, and other Hispanic. Hispanic origin is not a racial classification. Persons may be of any race and of Hispanic origin. Hispanic origin is used interchangeably with Spanish and Spanish origin.

HOME OWNERSHIP see **TENURE.**

HOSPITAL see **COMMUNITY HOSPITAL.**

HOSPITAL DAY

A hospital day is a night spent in a hospital by a person admitted as an inpatient.

HOUSEHOLD

The person or persons occupying a housing unit. There are two main types of households: family households, which consist of two or more persons related by birth, marriage, or adoption living together (see also **Family; Family Type**); and non-family households, which consist of a person living alone, or together with unrelated individuals (see Unrelated Individuals). See also **Householder.**

HOUSEHOLD INCOME see **INCOME.**

HOUSEHOLD TYPE see **HOUSEHOLD.**

HOUSEHOLDER

The person in whose name a housing unit is rented or owned.

HOUSING UNIT

A house, apartment, mobile home or trailer, group of rooms, or single room occupied as a separate living quarter, or, if vacant, intended for occupancy as a separate living quarter. Separate living quarters are those in which the occupants live and eat separately from any other persons in the building and which have direct access from the outside of the building or through a common hall.

Both occupied and vacant housing units are counted in many surveys; however, recreational vehicles, boats, caves, tents, railroad cars, and the like are only included if they are occupied as someone's usual place of residence. Vacant mobile homes are included if they are intended for occupancy on the site where they stand. Vacant mobile homes on dealer's sales lots, at the factory, or in storage yards are excluded.

Most housing unit data is for year-round housing units which comprises all occupied housing units plus vacant housing units intended for year round use. Vacant units held for seasonal use or migratory labor are excluded. See also **Occupancy Status, Rooms, Specified Owner-Occupied Housing Units, Tenure, Value (Housing).**

HOUSING TENURE see **TENURE.**

INCIDENT see **CRIME.**

INCOME

The term income has different definitions depending on how it is modified and in what situation it is used. Like many government statistical terms, income can be viewed hierarchically.

Personal income is the current income received by persons from all sources, minus their personal contributions for social insurance. Persons include individuals (including owners of unincorporated firms), non-profit institutions serving individuals, private trust funds, and private non-insured welfare funds. Personal income includes transfers (payments not resulting from current production) from government and business such as Social Security benefits, public assistance, etc., but excludes transfers among persons. Also included are certain non-monetary types of income, chiefly estimated net rental value to owner-occupants of their homes, the value of services furnished without payment by financial intermediaries, and food and fuel produced and consumed on farms.

Disposable personal income is personal income less personal tax and non-tax payments. It is income available to persons for spending and saving. Personal tax and non-tax payments are tax payments (net of refunds) by persons (excluding contributions for social insurance) that are not chargeable to business expenses, and certain personal payments to general government that are treated like taxes. Personal taxes include income, estate and gift, personal property, and motor vehicle licenses. Non-tax payments include passport fees, fines and penalties, donations, tuition and fees paid to schools and hospitals mainly operated by the government.

Money income is a smaller less inclusive category than personal income. Money income is the sum of the amounts received from wages and salaries, self-employment income (including losses), Social Security, Supplemental Security Income, public assistance, interest, dividends, rents, royalties, estate or trust income, veterans payments, unemployment and workers' compensation payments, private and government retirement and disability pensions, alimony, child support, and any other source of money income which was regularly received. Capital gains or losses and lump-sum or one-time payments, such as life insurance settlements, are excluded. Also excluded are non-cash benefits such as food stamps, health benefits, housing subsidies, rent-free housing, and the goods produced and consumed on farms. Money income is reported for households and various household types as well as for unrelated individuals. (In regard to family money income it should be noted that only the amount received by all family members 15 years old and over is counted, and excludes income received by household members not related to the householder.) It is reported in aggregate, median, mean, and per capita amounts. Money income is also used for determining the poverty status of families and unrelated individuals.

INFANT MORTALITY

The deaths of live-born children who do not reach their first birthday. Infant mortality is usually expressed as a rate per 1,000 live births.

INPATIENT DAYS (HOSPITALS)

The number of adult and pediatric days of care rendered during a given period. See also Hospital Day.

INSTITUTION OF HIGHER EDUCATION

An institution which offers programs of study beyond the secondary school level terminating in an associate, baccalaureate, or higher degree. See also **College; University.**

JAIL

A facility, usually operated by a local law enforcement agency, holding persons detained pending adjudication and/or persons committed after adjudication to a sentence of one year or less.

LABOR FORCE STATUS

A term which refers to whether or not a person is in the labor force, and, if in the labor force, whether he or she is employed or unemployed, a full-time worker or a part-time worker, etc. Persons are in the labor force if they are in the civilian labor force or in the Armed Forces.

The civilian labor force consists of both employed and unemployed persons, full-time and part-time workers. Generally, persons outside the labor force consist of full-time homemakers, students who do not work, retired persons, and inmates of institutions. "Discouraged workers," those who do not have a job and have not been seeking one, are also considered to be not in the labor force. See also **Civilian Labor Force.**

LARCENY see **CRIME.**

LIMITATION OF ACTIVITY see **HEALTH LIMITATION OF ACTIVITY.**

LIVE BIRTH

The live birth of an infant, defined as the complete expulsion or extraction from its mother of a product of conception, irrespective of the duration of the pregnancy, which, after such separation, breathes or shows any evidence of life such as heartbeat, umbilical cord pulsation, or definite movement of voluntary muscles, whether or not the umbilical cord has been cut or the placenta is attached. Each such birth is considered live born.

MARITAL STATUS

All persons 15 years of age and older are classified by the Bureau of the Census according to marital status. The Bureau defines two broad categories of marital status:

Single - all those persons who have never been married (including persons whose marriage has been annulled), and **Ever married** - which is composed of the now married, the widowed, and the divorced. **Now married** persons are those who are legally married (as well as some persons who have common law marriages, along with some unmarried couples who live together and report their marital status as married), and whose marriage has not ended by widowhood or divorce. The now married are sometimes further subdivided: married, spouse present; separated; married, spouse absent; married, spouse absent, other. **Married, spouse present** covers married couples living together. **Separated** includes those persons legally separated or otherwise absent from their spouse because of marital discord (such as persons who have been deserted or who have parted because they no longer want to live together but who have not obtained a divorce). Separated includes persons with a limited divorce. **Married, spouse absent** covers those households where the both the husband and the wife were not counted as members of the same household, (or where both husband and wife lived together in group quarters). **Married, spouse absent, other**, includes those married persons whose spouse was not counted as a member of the same household, besides those who are separated. Included are persons whose spouse was employed and living away from home, absent in the armed forces, or was an inmate of an institution. **Widowed** includes widows and widowers who have not remarried. **Divorced** includes persons who are legally divorced and have not remarried.

MARRIED COUPLES see **FAMILY TYPE.**

MARRIED PERSONS see **MARITAL STATUS.**

MEAN

The arithmetic average of a set of values. It is derived by dividing the sum of a group of numerical items by the total number of items. Mean income (of a population), for example, is defined as the value obtained by dividing the total or aggregate income by the population. Thus, the mean income for families is obtained by dividing the aggregate of all income reported by persons in families by the total number of families. See also **Median.**

MEDIAN

In general, a value that divides the total range of values into two equal parts. For example, to say that the median money income of families in the United States in 1985 was $27,735 indicates that half of all families had incomes larger than that value, and half had less. See also **Mean.**

MEDICAID

A federally funded but state administered and operated program which provides medical benefits to certain low income persons in need of medical care. The program, authorized in 1965 by Title XIX of the Social Security Act, categorically covers participants in the Aid to Families with Dependent Children (AFDC) program, as well as some participants in the Supplemental Security Income (SSI) program, along with those other people deemed medically needy in each participating state. Each state determines the benefits covered, rates of payment to providers, and methods of administering the program.

MEDICARE

A federally funded nationwide health insurance program providing health insurance protection to people 65 years of age and over, people eligible for social security disability payments for more than two years, and people with end-state renal disease, regardless of income. The program was enacted July 30, 1965, as title XVIII, Health Insurance for the Aged, of the Social Security Act, and became effective on July 1, 1966. It consists of two separate but coordinated programs: hospital insurance (Part A), and supplementary medical insurance (Part B).

METROPOLITAN AREA see CONSOLIDATED METROPOLITAN STATISTICAL AREA; METROPOLITAN STATISTICAL AREA; PRIMARY METROPOLITAN STATISTICAL AREA; STANDARD CONSOLIDATED STATISTICAL AREA; STANDARD METROPOLITAN STATISTICAL AREA

METROPOLITAN STATISTICAL AREA (MSA)

A geographic concept introduced in June, 1984, to replace the Standard Metropolitan Statistical Area (SMSA). In general, an MSA is a geographic area consisting of a large population nucleus, together with adjacent communities that have a high degree of economic and social integration with that nucleus. MSAs are designated in accordance with a detailed 16 section criteria established by the federal Office of Management and Budget (OMB). In general, MSAs are a county based concept which must include a city that, with contiguous, densely settled territory, constitutes a Census Bureau defined urbanized area having at least 50,000 population. (However, if an MSA's largest city has less than 50,000 population, the MSA as a whole must have a total population of at least 100,000). Adjacent MSAs are consolidated into a single MSA if certain conditions relating to commuting to work, size, and geographic proximity are met. See also **Consolidated Metropolitan Statistical Area; New England County Metropolitan Area; Primary Metropolitan Statistical Area.**

NEW ENGLAND COUNTY METROPOLITAN AREA (NECMA)

A geographic concept developed for the New England s.ates (Massachusetts, Connecticut, Rhode Island, Maine, New Hampshire, Vermont) to present data that is only available on a county-level basis . Unlike the rest of the country, Metropolitan Statistical Areas (MSAs) in the New England states are officially defined in terms of cities and towns instead of counties. As a result New England MSA data may not be directly comparable to MSA data in the rest of the country. NECMAs are county-based geographic areas (which follow the same general guidelines of MSAs in other parts of the country) and thus provide a basis of comparison with other states. NECMAs do not replace the MSAs in New England, but supplement them.

MOBILE HOME see HOUSING UNIT.

MONEY INCOME see **INCOME.**

MURDER see **CRIME.**

NATIONAL CRIME SURVEY

A twice yearly survey of 49,000 households comprising over 102,000 inhabitants 12 years of age and older. Administered by the Bureau of Justice Statistics, the survey measures criminal victimization by surveying victims directly. It differs from the FBI Uniform Crime Report (UCR) which is based on crimes reported to police. See also **Crime.**

NURSING HOME

A facility with three or more beds providing adults with nursing care and/or personal care (such as help with bathing, eating, using toilet facilities, or dressing) and/or supervision over such activities as money management, walking, and shopping.

OCCUPANCY STATUS (HOUSING)

The classification of all housing units as either occupied or vacant. **Occupied housing units** are those that have one or more persons living in them as their usual residence, and include units whose usual occupants are temporarily absent (e.g., on vacation). **Vacant housing units** are those that have no one living in them as their usual residence. Also classified as vacant are housing units that are temporarily occupied solely by persons who have a usual residence elsewhere, newly constructed units completed to the point where all exterior windows and doors are installed and final usable floors are in place, and vacant mobile homes or trailers intended to be occupied on the site on which they stand.

OCCUPATION

The kind of work a person does at a job or business. Occupation is reported for a given survey period, (most frequently the period covered by the survey, the reference period, is the week including March 12). If the person was not at work during the reference period, occupation usually refers to the person's most recent job or business. Persons working at more than one job are asked to identify the job at which he or she works the most hours, which is then counted as his or her occupation.

Occupations are classified according to the Standard Occupational Classification system (SOC), a system promulgated by the federal Office of Management and Budget.

OWNER OCCUPIED HOUSING UNIT see **TENURE.**

PART-TIME ENROLLMENT (HIGHER EDUCATION)

The number of students enrolled in higher education courses with a total credit load of less than 75% of the normal full-time credit load.

PART-TIME WORKERS see **CIVILIAN LABOR FORCE.**

PERSONAL INCOME see **INCOME.**

POPULATION

The number of inhabitants of an area. The total population of the United States is the sum of all persons living within the United States, plus all members of the Armed Forces living in foreign countries, Puerto Rico, Guam, and the U.S. Virgin Islands. Other Americans living abroad (e.g., civilian federal employees and dependents of members of the Armed Forces or other federal employees are not included).

The **resident population of the United States**, is the population living within the geographic United States. This includes members of the Armed Forces stationed in the United States and their families as well as foreigners working or studying here. It excludes foreign military, naval, and diplomatic personnel and their families located here and residing in embassies or similar quarters, as well as Americans living abroad. Resident population is often the denominator when calculating birth and death rates, incidence of disease, and other rates.

The **civilian population** is the resident population excluding members of the Armed Forces. However, families of members of the Armed Forces are included.

The **civilian non-institutional population** is the civilian population not residing in institutions. Institutions include, correctional institutions; detention homes and training schools for juvenile delinquents; homes for the aged and dependent (e.g., nursing homes and convalescent homes); homes for dependent and neglected children; homes and schools for the mentally and physically handicapped; homes for unwed mothers; psychiatric, tuberculosis, and chronic disease hospitals; and residential treatment centers.

POVERTY STATUS

Although the term poverty connotes a complex set of economic, social, and psychological conditions, the standard statistical definition provides for only estimates of economic poverty. These are based on the receipt of money income before taxes and exclude the value of government payments and transfers such as food stamps or Medicare; private transfers, such as health insurance premiums paid by employers; gifts; the depletion of assets; and borrowed money. Thus the term poverty as used by government agencies, classifies persons and families in relation to being above or below a specified income level, or poverty threshold. Those below this threshold are said to be in poverty, or more accurately, as below the poverty level. Poverty thresholds vary by size of family, number of children, and age of householder and are updated annually. Poverty status is also determined for unrelated individuals living in households, but not for those living in group quarters nor for persons in the Armed Forces. The poverty threshold is revised each year according to formula based on the Consumer Price Index.

PRIMARY METROPOLITAN STATISTICAL AREA (PMSA)

This geographic concept, introduced in June, 1984, combines with Metropolitan Statistical Area (MSA) and Consolidated Metropolitan Statistical Areas (CMSA), to replace the Standard Metropolitan Statistical Area (SMSA) concept. PMSAs are designated according to criteria established by the federal Office of Management and Budget. In general PMSAs are those counties with populations of at least 100,000 (60%

must be urban), in which less than 50% of its resident workers commute to jobs outside the county. PMSAs are parts of Consolidated Metropolitan Statistical Areas (CMSAs).

PRISON

A confinement facility having custodial authority over adults sentenced to confinement for a period of more than one year. Prisons are usually run by State or federal authorities.

PRIVATE SCHOOL see SCHOOL.

PROPERTY CRIME see CRIME.

PUBLIC SCHOOL see SCHOOL.

RACE

The Bureau of the Census in many of its surveys (most notably in the decennial censuses of population) asks all persons to identify themselves according to race. The concept of race as used by the Bureau reflects the self-identification of the respondents. It is not meant to denote any clear cut scientific or biological definition.

Although it is often reported with racial categories, **Hispanic origin**, or Spanish origin, is not a racial category. Persons may be of any race and of Hispanic origin. Those who describe themselves as Hispanic (or Mexican, Cuban, Chicano, etc.) in response to a question about race, are included by the Bureau in the racial classification, "other." See also **Hispanic Origin.**

RAPE see CRIME.

REFERENCE PERSON

Most frequently, the person who responds to a government survey. Most surveys done by the federal government are based on households and begin by asking the initial respondent the name of the person in whose name the housing unit is owned or rented (this person is designated as the householder). Usually the householder is the reference person. Other household members are defined in relation to the householder.

REGION

The Bureau of the Census has divided the United States into four regions. This division is the primary geographic subdivision of the nation for statistical reporting purposes. As a result, almost all federal agencies, along with many private data collectors, have adopted the regional subdivision and use it for presenting statistical data. The four regions are the **Northeast** (Maine, New Hampshire, Vermont, Massachusetts, Rhode Island, Connecticut, New York, New Jersey, Pennsylvania); the **Midwest** (Ohio, Indiana, Illinois, Michigan, Wisconsin, Minnesota, Iowa, Missouri, North Dakota, South Dakota, Kansas, Nebraska); the **South** (Delaware, Maryland, District of Columbia, Virginia, West Virginia, North Carolina, South Carolina, Georgia, Florida,

Kentucky, Tennessee, Alabama, Mississippi, Arkansas, Louisiana, Oklahoma, Texas); and the **West** (Montana, Idaho, Colorado, Wyoming, New Mexico, Arizona, Utah, Nevada, Washington, Oregon, California, Alaska, Hawaii). In this book, all regional data conform to this definition.

REGULAR SCHOOL see **SCHOOL**.

RENTER OCCUPIED HOUSING UNIT see **TENURE**.

RESIDENT POPULATION see **POPULATION**.

RESTRICTED-ACTIVITY DAY see **DISABILITY DAY**.

ROBBERY see **CRIME**.

ROOMS (HOUSING)

The number of whole rooms intended for living purposes in both occupied and vacant housing units. These rooms include living rooms, dining rooms, kitchens, bedrooms, finished recreation rooms, enclosed porches suitable for year-round use, and lodger's rooms. Excluded are strip or Pullman kitchens, bathrooms, open porches, balconies, foyers, halls, half-rooms, utility rooms, unfinished attics or basements, or other space used for storage. A partially divided room, such as a dinette next to a kitchen or living room, is a separate room only if there is a partition from floor to ceiling, but not if the partition consists solely of shelves or cabinets.

RURAL see **URBAN/RURAL POPULATION**.

SCHOOL

Elementary and secondary schools are divisions of the school system consisting of students in one or more grade groups or other identifiable groups, organized as one unit with one or more teachers giving instruction of a defined type, and housed in a school plant of one or more buildings. More than one school may be housed in one school plant as is the case where elementary and secondary programs are housed in the same building.

Regular schools generally are those which advance a person toward a diploma or degree. They include public and private nursery schools, kindergartens, graded schools, colleges, universities, and professional schools.

Public schools are controlled and supported by local, state, or federal government agencies.

Private schools are controlled and supported mainly by religious organizations, private persons, or private organizations.

SCHOOL ENROLLMENT see **ENROLLMENT**.

SCHOOL-LOSS DAY see **DISABILITY DAY**.

SELF-EMPLOYMENT INCOME

    A type of money income which comprises net income (gross receipts minus operating expenses) received by persons from an unincorporated business, profession, and/or from the operation of a farm as a farm owner, tenant, or sharecropper. See also **Money Income.**

SEPARATED PERSONS see **MARITAL STATUS.**

SERIOUS CRIME see **CRIME.**

SINGLE PERSON HOUSEHOLDS see **HOUSEHOLD.**

SINGLE PERSONS see **MARITAL STATUS.**

SPECIFIED OWNER-OCCUPIED HOUSING UNITS

    Specified owner-occupied units are single family houses on less than ten acres, which have no commercial enterprise or medical practice on the property. Excluded are owner-occupied condominium housing units, mobile homes, trailers, boats, tents, or vans occupied as a usual residence as well as owner-occupied non-condominium units in multi-family buildings. See also **Housing Unit.**

STANDARD CONSOLIDATED STATISTICAL AREA (SCSA)

    A large concentration of metropolitan population composed of two or more contiguous Standard Metropolitan Statistical Areas (SMSAs) which together meet certain criteria of population size, urban character, social and economic integration, and/or contiguity of urbanized areas. Each SCSA must have a population of one million or more. The SCSA concept was replaced with the new metropolitan area classifications in June, 1984. See Consolidated Metropolitan Statistical Area; Metropolitan Statistical Area; Primary Metropolitan Statistical Area.

STANDARD METROPOLITAN STATISTICAL AREA (SMSA)

    A geographic area concept used until 1984. In general, an SMSA is a large population nucleus and nearby communities which have a high degree of economic and social integration within that nucleus. Each SMSA consists of one or more entire counties (or county equivalents) that meet certain criteria of population, commuting ties, and metropolitan character. In New England, towns and cities rather than counties are the basic units and count as county equivalents. An SMSA includes a city and, generally, the entire surrounding urbanized area and the remainder of the county or counties in which the urbanized area is located. An SMSA also includes those additional outlying counties which meet specified criteria relating to metropolitan character and level of commuting ties.

    The SMSA concept was developed in 1949 and has been refined for each succeeding decennial census since 1950. In June, 1984, SMSAs were superseded by three new metropolitan area concepts: Metropolitan Statistical Areas (MSAs), Consolidated

Metropolitan Statistical Areas (CMSAs), and Primary Metropolitan Statistical Areas (PMSAs).

TAXES

Compulsory contributions exacted by a government for public purposes (except employee and employer assessments for retirement and social insurance purposes, which are classified as insurance trust revenue). All tax revenue is classified as general revenue and comprises amounts received (including interest and penalties, but excluding protested amounts and refunds) from all taxes imposed by a government.

TENURE

A concept relating to housing units. All occupied housing units are classified as being either owner-occupied or renter occupied. A housing unit is owner-occupied if the owner or co-owner lives in the unit even if the unit is mortgaged or not fully paid for. All other housing units are considered to be renter occupied, regardless of whether or not cash rent is paid for them by a member of the household. See also **Housing Unit.**

UNEMPLOYED PERSONS see CIVILIAN LABOR FORCE.

UNEMPLOYMENT see CIVILIAN LABOR FORCE.

UNIFORM CRIME REPORTING (UCR) PROGRAM

A program administered by the FBI which collects reports from most police agencies in the nation (covering approximately 95% of the population) on serious crimes known to police (violent crime and property crime), arrests, police officers and related items. The Bureau issues monthly and annual summary reports based on the program. See also **Crime.**

UNIVERSITY

An institution of higher education consisting of a liberal arts college, a diverse graduate program, and usually two or more professional schools or faculties and empowered to confer degrees in various fields of study. See also **Higher Education.**

UNRELATED INDIVIDUAL

An unrelated individual is generally a person living in a household, and is either: 1) a householder living alone or only with persons who are not related to him or her by blood, marriage, or adoption, or; 2) a roomer, boarder, partner, roommate, or resident employee unrelated to the householder. Certain persons living in group quarters (who are not inmates of institutions) are also counted as unrelated individuals.

URBAN/RURAL POPULATION

Urban and rural are type of area concepts rather than specific areas outlined on maps. The urban population comprises all persons living in urbanized areas and in places of 2,500 or more inhabitants outside urbanized areas. The rural population consists of everyone else. Therefore, a rural classification need not imply a farm or sparsely settled areas, since a small city or town is rural when it is outside an urbanized area and has fewer than 2,500 inhabitants. The terms urban and rural are independent of metropolitan and non-metropolitan; both urban and rural areas occur inside and outside metropolitan areas. See also **Urbanized Area.**

URBANIZED AREA

A population concentration of at least 50,000 inhabitants, generally consisting of a central city and the surrounding, closely settled, contiguous territory (suburbs). The urbanized area criteria define a boundary based on a population density of at least 1,000 persons per square mile, but also include some less densely settled areas, such as industrial parks and railroad yards, if they are within areas of dense urban development. The density level of 1,000 persons per square mile corresponds approximately to the contiguously built-up area around a city or cities. The urban fringe is that part of the urbanized area outside of a central city or cities.

Typically, an entire urbanized area is included within an Standard Metropolitan Statistical Area (SMSA) or Metropolitan Statistical Area (MSA). The SMSA (or MSA) is usually much larger in terms of area and includes territory where the population density is less than 1,000. Occasionally more than one urbanized area is located within an SMSA (MSA). In some cases a small part of an urbanized area may extend beyond an SMSA (MSA) boundary, or possibly into an adjacent SMSA (MSA). Urbanized areas sometimes cross state boundaries as well.

VACANCY STATUS see OCCUPANCY STATUS.

VALUE (HOUSING UNITS)

In surveys done by the Bureau of the Census, the value of owner-occupied housing units is the respondent's estimate of the current dollar worth of the property; for vacant units, the value is the price asked for the property. A property is defined as the house and the land on which it stands. Respondents are asked by the Bureau to estimate the value of the house and land even if they own only the house, or own the house jointly. Statistics for value are only gathered by the Bureau for owner-occupied condominium units and for specified owner-occupied units (single family houses on less than ten acres, and with no business on the property).

VICTIMIZATION see CRIME.

VIOLENT CRIME see CRIME.

VOTING AGE POPULATION

All persons over the age of 18 (the voting age for federal elections) in a given geographic area comprise the voting age population. The voting age population does include a small number of persons who, although of voting age, are not eligible to vote (e.g. resident aliens, inmates of institutions, etc.). The voting age population is estimated in even numbered years by the Bureau of the Census.

WAGES AND SALARIES

Wages and salaries are a type (subgroup) of money income and include civilian wages and salaries, Armed Forces pay and allowances, piece-rate payments, commissions, tips, National Guard or Reserve pay (received for training periods), and cash bonuses before deductions for taxes, pensions, union dues, etc. See also **Money Income.**

WIDOWED PERSONS see **MARITAL STATUS.**

WORK DISABILITY

A health condition which limits the kind or amount of work a person can do, or prevents working at a job. A person is limited in the kind of work he or she can do if the person has a health condition which restricts his or her choice of jobs. A person is limited in amount of work if he or she is not able to work at a full-time (35 hours or more per week) job or business. See also **Condition (Health).**

WORK-LOSS DAY see **DISABILITY DAY.**

Index